FESTIVAL OF FIRE

Series No. 5

FOUNDATIONS OF A BLESSED FAMILY

10 Principles You Need

Godson T. Nembo

CRNPUBLICATIONS®   IEM PRESS

FOUNDATIONS OF A BLESSED FAMILY:
10 Principles You Need

Copyright @ September 2025
Godson T. Nembo

ISBN: 978-1-63603-327-3

Published in Cameroon by
Christian Restoration Network (CRN) Publications
P.O. BOX 31339 Yaounde – Cameroon

IEM PRESS is honored to present this title with the author. The views expressed or implied in this work are those of the author. IEM Press provides our imprint seal representing design excellence, creative content and high quality production. To learn more about IEM Press visit www.iempublishing.com

All scripture quotations are from the New King James Version (NKJV) of the Bible, except otherwise stated.

For more information:
www.christianrestorationnetwork.org
www.facebook.com/godsontnembo
Email: contact@christianrestorationnetwork.org

Or write to:
Tangumonkem Godson Nembo
P.O. Box 31339 Biyem Assi Yaounde – Cameroon
Tel: (237) 652.382.693 or 696.565.864

Prayer Storm Online Store:
With MTN or Orange Mobile Money *(for those in Cameroon)* and E-Wallet *(for those abroad)*, you can easily obtain the electronic version of this book and other CRN publications via www.amazon.com at
https://shorturl.at/pqxyT or
www.christianrestorationnetwork.org/our-bookstore.
https://goo.gl/ktf3rT
Contact (237) 679.465.717 or
prayerstorm@christianrestorationnetwork.org

Cover Design: Tangu Monkem (237) 671.331.222
Layout: IEM Press (237) 672.827.784

How to Use this Book

Carefully read these instructions before you start praying with this book.

1) *Read the message of the day* and all the scriptures before you start praying.

2) *Use the prayer points provided at the end of each chapter as a guide,* but depend on the Holy Spirit to reveal more.

3) *Pray all the prayers audibly* and not in your heart. Don't disturb anybody.

4) *Take time and pray through each prayer point before you move* to the next one.

5) *If you can, always pray in tongues* as you pray with this book.

6) *Pause and listen to God* as you pray because He has many things to reveal to you.

7) *If you are following the 30-day program, read and pray with each chapter for 3 days.* Divide the prayer points as you wish.

8) *Write down your prayer topics to pray during the fast.*

9) *As led by the Holy Spirit, you can also select topics* from this book to carry out a 1 day, 3 days, 7 days, 21 days, or even 40 days fast.

10) Pastors, prayer cell leaders, ministry heads, etc., can use this book to lead their Churches or groups for a season of fasting and prayer.

11) *You can still pray without fasting* if your health condition does not permit you to fast now.

Table of Contents

Introduction

"If the foundations are destroyed, what can the righteous do?"
(Psalm 11:3).

After more than 29 years of pastoral ministry, I have watched too many families suffer needlessly. They love God, pray and fast, yet remain stuck in cycles of conflict, poverty, and spiritual bondage. Why? Because while many seek deliverance, few know how to build lasting, godly foundations.

I've also witnessed how false teachings keep families in bondage. Teachings like:

"Break the curse, and everything will be fine."

"Just sow a seed and your family will prosper."

"Only the man of God can set your family free."

These teachings often leave believers dependent and powerless. Yet Scripture says,

"My people are destroyed for lack of knowledge" (Hosea 4:6). Beloved in the Lord, d**eliverance is not the destination; it's the starting point. True transformation begins when you build.**

So, what is *'The Blessing'*? It's not just wealth or comfort. In everyday terms, it's the visible presence of God's favor – peace, provision, purpose, and generational continuity. The Hebrew word *'Barak'* means "To empower, enrich, and multiply." The Greek *'Eulogeo'* speaks of "Being spoken well of, favored, and prospered."

What is a "Blessed Family?" It is a family empowered by God to succeed, flourish, and fulfill divine purpose – spiritually, relationally, emotionally, and materially. A blessed family enjoys seven marks: God's presence, fruitfulness, provision, protection, generational impact, unity, and kingdom relevance.

Some families are sitting on broken or demonic foundations – ancestral altars, occultic ties, sexual perversion, or bloodline curses, etc. Others are failing because of ignorance, rebellion, or misplaced priorities.

A house cannot stand if its foundation is cracked or compromised. But here's the good news: no matter your past, a new foundation can be laid in Christ.

In this book, I will walk you through ten critical foundations that every family must intentionally build to experience God's blessing. Each chapter will expose both the biblical blueprint and real-life examples – families that prospered by following divine principles, and others that collapsed by ignoring them. You will also find instructions, prayer topics, and prophetic declarations to align your spirit and intercede for your family. This book is not just for reading; it is a manual for family transformation.

Maybe your family history is one of pain, poverty, or confusion. Maybe your parents or grandparents didn't know the truth. But now, you do. You cannot continue as they did. You must become the agent of change. You are not just reading a book—you are stepping into a divine assignment. The healing of your family begins with you.

This book was prayerfully written to commemorate the 25th anniversary of the 30 Days Annual Fast organized by Christian Restoration Network (CRN), under the prophetic theme: "O LORD, BLESS MY FAMILY." The fast has become a life-changing season of restoration for individuals and households across nations. As you read this book during the fast, or as part of your personal spiritual journey, expect to encounter God's power. Expect chains to break, marriages to be healed, prodigal children to return, and long-standing evil altars to crumble.

Read, pray, fast, and build!
"In you, all the families of the earth shall be blessed"
(Genesis 12:3).

Pastor Godson T. Nembo
Yaounde, August 17, 2025

A Survey Report – "A Blessed Family"

This report summarizes the key insights from 76 individuals who responded to a survey exploring the meaning of a "Blessed family."

Question 1: What is a Blessed Family?
Respondents strongly agreed that **"A blessed family is one centered on God."** Such a family lives by biblical values, prays together, and places Jesus Christ as the foundation. Being "blessed" is not defined by material wealth but by spiritual alignment and inner peace.

A blessed family has the following characteristics: God-Centeredness, love & unity, prosperity in all areas, divine protection & favor, and generational blessings.

Sample definitions from respondents:
- "A family that lives in the fear of God and meditates on His Word."
- "A home that mirrors Christ's character daily."
- "A peaceful, joyful, and humble environment rooted in love."

Question 2: Is Your Family Blessed?
Results:
- Yes – 82%
- No – 16%
- Partially – 2%

Most felt their families were blessed but noted ongoing challenges and spiritual growth in progress.

Question 3: What Contributes to a Blessed Family?
Respondents attributed their blessings to spiritual practices, not circumstances.

Key contributors:

- *Faith in God:* A strong relationship with Jesus.
- *Prayer and Scripture:* Regular family prayer and meditation on the Word.
- *Parental Influence:* The role of praying parents, especially mothers, in establishing spiritual foundations.
- *Obedience:* Commitment to biblical values and surrendering to God's will.

Question 4: What Hinders a Family from Being Blessed?

Respondents who answered "No" cited spiritual and relational issues. *Barriers included:*

- *Negative Spiritual Roots:* Idolatry, witchcraft, generational curses.
- *Division:* Conflict, disunity, and lack of shared faith.
- *Personal Sin:* Pride, immorality, and unforgiveness.
- *Lack of Spiritual Leadership:* Absent or spiritually passive parents.

Question 5: Do You Admire a Family in Your Community?

- Yes – 82%

These families were admired for serving God together, maintaining unity, and living in peace and godly order.

Question 6: How Can a Family Become Blessed?

Respondents shared a clear biblical roadmap:

- Make Jesus the foundation.
- Obey God's Word (Joshua 1:8).
- Build a strong prayer life.
- Fulfill biblical roles within the home.
- Raise children in the Lord.
- Live in love, humility, and forgiveness.
- Evangelize and pray for family members (Acts 16:31).

The Need For This Book:

Before writing this book, I sensed the need to pause and listen. I didn't want to simply present my own ideas. I wanted to understand the hearts of families today. So, I conducted a survey, asking direct and honest questions about what people desire most in a family and what they believe truly makes a family "blessed."

The response was both overwhelming and eye-opening. More than 75 people from diverse backgrounds poured out their hearts. A consistent truth emerged: "A blessed family is not defined by wealth, comfort, or a trouble-free life. Instead, it is a family deeply rooted in Jesus Christ – one that fears God and lives in love, peace, and unity."

Yet, many admitted they felt hindered from experiencing this reality. They spoke of generational patterns, spiritual battles, division, and the lack of practical guidance. The vision was clear, but the pathway seemed hidden.

This book is written as a direct response to that longing. The survey confirmed that while most families know what they desire, many struggle to cultivate it in daily life. The ten foundational principles you will discover here are not theories but practical, biblical keys designed to bridge the gap between the family you have and the one God intends you to build.

Chapter 1
Days 1-3

A Covenant With God

"My covenant I will not break, Nor alter the word that has gone out of My lips" (Psalm 89:34).

B reaking evil covenants is not enough to give you access to God's redemptive blessings. In fact, engaging in spiritual warfare to free yourself from satanic covenants is step one in the process. You must move to step two, which is establishing a covenant with God. You must develop a covenant mentality. You must also labor to bring your family members to embrace God's covenant, to free your family from the torments of evil covenants. Every family that is enjoying God's blessings has a covenant relationship with the living God.

Let me also underline here that it is not enough to claim Bible promises merely; you must commit yourself to meeting the requirements for the manifestation of each promise in your life and family. Did you know that each promise in the Bible has conditions attached to it? Check it out! To claim promises and refuse to meet the requirements is like expecting water to flow into your cup when the tap is not open. The covenant is about believing, saying, and doing God's Word.

The Story of Lott Carey

Lott Carey was America's first Black missionary to Africa and a true pioneer of faith. Born into slavery, he rose above his circumstances through a covenant mentality.

At age 24, in 1804, Carey heard the Gospel in a Baptist church and gave his life to Christ. Though he was illiterate, his determination drove him to learn to read and study the Bible. His preaching soon had a profound impact on both Black and white audiences, and he felt a strong calling to take the Gospel to Africa.

Still a slave, Carey founded the African Missionary Society to execute this vision. By 1813, he had saved enough to purchase freedom for himself and his two children, demonstrating both his devotion to family and his belief in a better future.

He later led the first Baptist missionary team to Africa, helping to establish the colony of Liberia. In Monrovia, he founded a Baptist church and played a key role in the community's spiritual and social development. Carey was known not only for his preaching but also for his work in education and healthcare.

He died at 48, but left a powerful legacy of faith, leadership, and service. Lott Carey's life proves how far unwavering faith and dedication can take someone, even from the chains of slavery to history-making mission work. He is an epitome of a man whose covenant walk with God brought a tremendous blessing to his family and generation.

What is a Covenant?

The term "Covenant" comes from the Latin word *'Con venire,'* which means "A coming together." It presupposes two or more parties who come together to make a contract, agreeing on promises, stipulations, privileges, and responsibilities. In political situations, it can be translated as a treaty. In business, it is a contract.[1] Marriage is also a covenant.

One who is in a covenant with God is a believer who has entered into a deep and unshakable relationship with God by placing their faith in what Jesus did on the cross. This person understands what it means to fully surrender to Jesus and follow Him with all their heart. They have also made a clear choice to live with a Kingdom mindset – putting God's ways and His purpose first in every area of their life. This is the mentality you need to raise a blessed family. It is a covenant mentality.

You Need A Covenant Mentality

It takes a covenant mentality to walk with God and enjoy His blessings. You need a covenant mentality to influence your unbelieving family to abandon their idols and sinful ways and become disciples of Jesus Christ. What is a covenant mentality?

1. It is a "God-only" Mentality

A "God-only mentality" means placing complete trust in God above all else. You believe that only God can truly guide, provide, protect, and give you purpose. Your confidence is not in people, money, or your strength, but in God alone. One lesson God has been teaching me all these years is to trust Him to solve all my problems and not rely on any human being. People can frustrate you with false promises.

One with a God-only mentality serves God and Him alone. When God gave the Ten Commandments, He told the children of Israel,

"You shall have no other gods before me" (Exodus 20:3).

Throughout the Bible, God's main issue with Israel was idolatry. He consistently called them to be faithful to Him alone, remembering His covenant and serving Him with all their heart, mind, and strength.

Abraham is a model of a God-only mentality.

"By faith Abraham obeyed... not knowing where he was going" (Hebrews 11:8).

He trusted God above comfort, logic, and even family. He believed the impossible and was willing to sacrifice his beloved son, Isaac, to honor God (Genesis 15, 22).

Today, many families are religious but not spiritual. They mix Christianity with idol worship – praying at family shrines one day, then attending church the next. This syncretism is weakening the spiritual foundation of many African Christian families and attracting curses.

The Bible is clear: you cannot serve God and idols.

"My beloved, flee from idolatry" (1 Corinthians 10:14).

God demands full consecration and devotion. Stop provoking His wrath through syncretism and hypocrisy. Apostle Paul warns,

"You cannot drink the cup of the Lord and the cup of demons. You cannot partake of the table of the Lord and the table of demons. Shall we provoke the Lord to jealousy? Are we stronger than he? (1 Corinthians 10:21-22).

If you want your family to walk in God's blessings, you must first separate yourself from idols and fully commit to the Living God. Then lead your family to do the same. God blesses those who serve Him wholeheartedly, just as Abraham did.

2. It is a "God-first" Mentality

A "God-first mentality" means putting God at the center of everything in your life. It's choosing to honor, seek, and obey God before anything else – your desires, plans, relationships, money, or even your comfort. It means God comes first in every decision, every priority, and every part of your day. Jesus described the God-first mentality clearly in Matthew 6:33:

"But seek first the Kingdom of God and His righteousness, and all these things will be given to you as well."

Abraham became a channel of transgenerational blessings to his family because he had a God-first mentality. Even though the command was painful, he was willing to sacrifice his beloved son Isaac because obeying God was top priority for him (Genesis 22). That day, God made a firm promise to bless his family.

"I will surely bless you, and I will surely multiply your offspring as the stars of heaven and as the sand that is on the seashore. And your offspring shall possess the gate of his enemies, and in your offspring shall all the nations of the earth be blessed, because you have obeyed my voice" (Genesis 22:17-18).

God imputed the grace for multiplication and dominion on Abraham's family line. Generations down the line, we see the power of the blessing at work in the lives of the children of Israel everywhere they went.

Your obedience to God today shapes the future of your family. The place you give to God now determines where your family will be tomorrow. I've never seen anyone put God first and end up last.

In 1988, my father, Pa A.T. Lekunze, was leading a church building project. Although he had begun building his own house, he suspended the project and said, *"I will build God's house, and He will build mine."* After completing the church project, he went on and built his house. Today, his children are living testimonies of how God can bless the family of a man who puts God first.

When I began the Full Gospel Mission Cow Street project in Bamenda in 2014, I wrote the exact words on the blueprint: *"Build God's house, and He will build yours."* That principle has shaped my life. On launch day, I gave my only car to the project because I believed in what my father lived by: put God first, and He will take care of the rest.

3.   It is a "God Cannot Fail" Mentality

The "God cannot fail" mentality is the unshakable belief that God always keeps His promises, never loses a battle, never makes a mistake, and never abandons His people. It means fully trusting that, no matter how complex or delayed things may seem, God will come through for you, because He is faithful, all-powerful, and perfect in all He does. It's not just confidence in what God can do, but also in the truth that He never fails to do what He says He will do.

After serving God for several years, Joshua boldly testified about God's unflinching faithfulness.

"Not one of all the Lord's good promises to Israel failed; everyone was fulfilled" (Joshua 21:45).

All the promises they had received through Moses were fulfilled as Joshua served God with a "God cannot fail" mentality. He led the people of Israel to possess their inheritance in the Promised Land.

Jesus faced death with the mentality that God cannot fail. He trusted His Father's plan would not fail. That is why he prayed,

"Father, into Your hands I commit my spirit" (Luke 23:46).

The covenant mentality that God cannot fail will help you trust God, regardless of the situation. You will not panic when things are delayed or become tough. You will live with unshakable faith, knowing God's plan will prevail.

This is the mindset you need to influence and disciple your family to God. If your conviction and commitment are shallow, you will not be able to influence and disciple your family to God. This may be the reason why your impact as a Christian on your family is almost zero. Let me ask you: "How firm is your conviction about God's faithfulness to fulfill His Word in your life and family?" Do you know that the depth of your conviction about God's faithfulness affects everything you do and those around you? Every family needs someone with the "God cannot fail" mentality to inspire them to become disciples of Christ.

4. It is An "If God Has Said It, I Will Do It" Mentality

This mindset means total trust and prompt obedience to God, even when it's complex, risky, or unclear. You don't wait for complete understanding to do what God has commanded you to do. It is an action mentality. If God has spoken, you move immediately.

Abraham obeyed God's call to leave everything at the age of 75 (Genesis 12:1-5). He had no church, no Bible, no pastor, just God's Word. His obedience blessed his generations and the entire world. Like Abraham, will you go out as a missionary at 75?

Noah built the ark before rain had ever fallen. He didn't ask for proof. For 120 years, he followed God's command despite public mockery. His obedience saved his family from the devastating flood (Hebrews 11:7).

My father lived this mindset. In 1982, he resigned from his teaching position at the Presbyterian Mission School in Batchuontai, Mamfe, because his superiors did not want him to practice his faith freely. We left our free home on the school campus, moved into a cramped rented room and parlor, with a family of eight. Those days were difficult. We survived by farming. The following year, I passed the Government Common Entrance exam in class six, but I was unable to continue to secondary school due to a lack of funds. Dad fasted and prayed, trusting God to provide a government job. In 1984, he was recruited by the government, just before several mission schools shut down. Many lost jobs, but his obedience opened a door that secured our future.

Peter left his fishing business when Jesus said, ***"Follow Me" (Matthew 4:19).*** That one act of obedience changed Church history. If you want your family to walk in God's blessing, obey His voice quickly and fully, even when it's hard. If God said it, do it!

A Covenant-Keeping God

God is the God of the Covenant. He is a Covenant Keeper, not a covenant breaker. His strength is in His inability to lie. God's Covenant is as solid as the earth and as rigid as the night and day rhythm (Jeremiah 33:19-21,25).

Psalm 89:34 says,

"I will not violate my covenant or alter the word that went forth from my lips."

God is faithful to His promises and committed to His covenant. He not only keeps covenant with His immediate covenant partners but also with their succeeding generations. Your covenant with God does not end with you; it continues with your generation. That is the mystery of Israel today; the covenant of God with Abraham, Isaac, and Jacob implicated them for generational blessings. Covenant has the power to stand the test of time and seasons.

God Relates With Us Through Covenants

God is not just interested in individuals; He makes covenants with families. From Abraham to the early church, we see a pattern: when one person enters into a covenant with God, the blessing is intended to flow down to their children and subsequent generations.

In our covenant relationship, God **promises blessings** and expects our **obedience** in return. Under the **Old Covenant** (Old Testament), Israel was required to follow three types of laws:

- **Moral laws** – right and wrong behavior
- **Ceremonial laws** – religious rituals
- **Civil laws** – social order and justice

Although they were saved by grace through faith in God's promises, especially the coming Messiah, their faith was demonstrated through obedience and sacrifices that pointed to Christ. Yet, no one at that time could keep the law perfectly. Paul summarizes it in Romans 3:23:

"For all have sinned and fall short of the glory of God."

So, God gave us a **New Covenant (New Testament)** – a better way. Through **Jesus Christ**, who lived a perfect life and died for our sins, the Old Covenant was fulfilled. Now, we are saved not by works, but by grace, through **faith in Him – the finished work of the cross (Ephesians 2:8)**.

But grace doesn't cancel obedience; it **empowers it.** Grace is never a license to sin; it empowers us to say no to sin and the works of the flesh (Titus 2:11-12). Jesus said,

"If you love me, keep my commandments" (John 14:15).

"Blessed are those who hear the Word and obey it" (Luke 11:28).

Jesus commands us to walk in purity, integrity, and honesty, just as He does. Those who do so enjoy more of His blessings.

However, you must know that obedience is a journey, not a destination of perfection. As we grow in faith, we also grow in obedience, experiencing God's peace, joy, and purpose. Now, through Christ, you are a **covenant** child of God (Ephesians 1:5). His promises to Abraham are yours (Galatians 3:13-14, 29). You are blessed, seated with Christ, and never alone (Ephesians 1:3; 2:6; Matthew 28:20).

Live with this conviction and become an instrument of significant impact in your family and community.

The Law of the Superior Covenant

"Jesus, our High Priest, has been given a ministry far superior to the old... He is the one who mediates for us a far better covenant with God, based on better promises" (Hebrews 8:6 NLT).

God has established a superior covenant with us through Jesus Christ – one that surpasses the Old Covenant in every way. Unlike the Old Covenant, which was based on laws, rituals, and animal sacrifices, the New Covenant is based on grace, love, and the blood of Jesus. It offers forgiveness, eternal life, and a personal relationship with God.

The law of the superior covenant is this: when a higher covenant is established, the lower one loses its power. Just as a legal marriage overrides a former engagement, the covenant you now have in Christ cancels every evil covenant, whether inherited, initiated, or imposed.

You are now Christ's own: His bride (2 Corinthians 11:2), His temple (1 Corinthians 3:16), and a member of His body (1 Corinthians 12:27). No demon, curse, or "Spirit spouse" has legal ground in your life. You are hidden in Christ (Colossians 3:3).

When spiritual attacks arise, don't panic, plead the blood, declare your covenant with Christ, and stand firm in the truth. Jesus cannot share His bride with Satan.

The Blessing of Walking in God's Covenant

God is a Covenant Keeper. Once your responsibility is discharged, God's response is guaranteed. Just do the one you are supposed to do, and God will do what He has promised to do.

When you walk in covenant with God – obeying His Word, living by faith, and honoring His commands, God blesses not only you but also your descendants. God promised this in Exodus 20:6, when he made a covenant with the nation of Israel.

"But showing love to a thousand generations of those who love Me and keep My commandments."

Proverbs 20:7 reechoes the same promise.

"The righteous man walks in his integrity; his children are blessed after him."

This shows us that being faithful to God's covenant produces a ripple effect; God's blessing flows through your family.

In 2 Samuel 7:12-16, God established a transgenerational covenant with David's family because of his passion to build God's house. God promised to establish his family line forever. As you read through the Bible, you see how God showed his descendants mercy for David's sake. This covenant preserved David's family until the birth of Jesus Christ.

The Philippian Jailer asked Paul how to be saved, and the Apostle told him:

"Believe in the Lord Jesus, and you will be saved—you and your household" (Acts 16:31).

His faith played a crucial role in the salvation of his entire family. Are you saved? You are key to a tremendous transformation in your family. Begin to see yourself as such, instead of believing the lie of the devil that your destiny and those of your family members are locked up in a pot, under a tree somewhere. God has saved you to save them. He has blessed you in Christ to be a blessing to them.

Covenant People Enjoy God's Secrets

Psalm 25:14 says,

> *"The LORD is a friend to those who fear him. He teaches them his covenant" (NLT).*

God offers deep, lasting friendship to those who honor, revere, and obey Him. What earthly friendship can compare to being a friend of the Creator of the universe?

The above verse in the New King James Version says,

> *"The secret of the Lord is with those who fear Him."*

True success has a secret, and God reveals it to those who walk in covenant with Him. As you worship, serve, and obey Him daily, your friendship with God grows, and so does His guidance in your life. He doesn't just guide spiritually – He gives insight for innovation, problem-solving, and creativity in every field.

Here are examples of individuals who tapped into divine inspiration:

- **Isaac Newton** – A devout Christian scientist who discovered gravity, formulated the laws of motion, and invented the reflecting telescope. He credited his discoveries to God's guidance.

- **Johannes Kepler** – Known for the laws of planetary motion, he believed God revealed the order of the universe to him.

- **Johann Sebastian Bach** – One of the greatest composers in history, he signed many of his works with *"Soli Deo Gloria"*—to the glory of God alone.

- **Elias Howe** – Invented the sewing machine after God gave him a dream, in which he was taken captive by savages and forced to watch them dance around him with spears that had holes in the tips. This dream inspired him to place the eye of the needle at the point, rather than the traditional position at the other end. He invented the lockstitch sewing machine, which revolutionized the textile industry.

As you commit yourself to walking in God's covenant, He will begin to share insights that will transform your life and even your generation.

When You Break God's Covenant (*Psalm 89:38-45*)
Rejecting God's covenant and living in disobedience while claiming to love Him brings serious consequences. Here are four results of turning away from God:

1) Loss of Protection and Blessing
"You have broken down his walls…" (v. 40)
When you walk in sin, your spiritual walls collapse. You become vulnerable to satanic attacks and defeat.

2) Shame and Humiliation
"All who pass by have plundered him…" (v. 41)
Families without a covenant with God often suffer public shame and destruction. Evil covenants with demonic forces bring curses, not solutions. No amount of prayer or fasting can rectify this situation until you renounce evil and return to God.

3) Loss of Joy and Strength
"You have strengthened his enemies…" (v. 42)
When you reject God's covenant, you lose spiritual strength. Enemies rise, and confusion, division, and sorrow invade your family. Only restoring your covenant with God can reverse this.

4) Darkness and Despair
"You have turned back his sword…" (v. 44)
Living in sin exposes you to spiritual darkness. Some families, in desperation, turn to witchcraft for help, making deadly pacts with demons. Only Jesus offers true, lasting freedom.

The Covenant Practice of Giving (Sowing) and Receiving (Reaping)

Giving and receiving is an unbreakable law of God. You cannot reverse the law of sowing and reaping. Jesus said in Luke 6:38,

> *"Give, and it will be given to you. Good measure, pressed down, shaken together, running over, will be put into your lap. For with the measure you use it will be measured back to you."*

Even unbelievers say, "Givers never lack." They consistently receive back.

In Genesis 8:22, God says,

> *"While the earth remains, seedtime and harvest, cold and heat, summer and winter, day and night, shall not cease."*

If you sow faithfully, you will surely reap a harvest. But don't forget what Paul teaches us in 2 Corinthians 9:6,

> *"Whoever sows sparingly will also reap sparingly, and whoever sows bountifully will also reap bountifully."*

Your harvest is always proportionate to the seed sown.

But receiving always precedes giving. God will not ask you to give what He has not given you. Beloved, He owns the earth, all that is in it, and all that you have (Psalm 24:1). We brought nothing to this world. We meet everything when we arrive, and we will take nothing with us when we leave this world. God owns the energy and strength we use to achieve anything (Psalm 18:1, 2, 27:1). God owns the favors and the opportunities that give us everything (Ecclesiastes 9:11; Exodus 12:36; 1 Corinthians 4:7). What determines your results is not your power, skill or connections but God's mercy. For example, you cannot make the right choices without God's help. He possesses the wisdom and expertise that have brought us wealth (Daniel 2:20, 21; John 3:27). You must recognize and honor Him.

Some Examples of Givers

- Adam gave his rib and received a beautiful wife, Eve (Genesis 2:21-22).
- God multiplied the meal for the widow of Zarephath, who gave to the man of God, Elijah (1 Kings 17:13-16).

- Jesus multiplied five loaves and two fishes from the boy, and fed 5,000 men besides women and children (John 6:11-12).

Lessons:

- What God takes from you is not to meet His need; it is geared towards meeting your need.
- What you release to God is far less compared to what God returns to you.
- What you give to God does not get lost; it is only multiplied and returned into your future.
- God takes what you have to give you what you need.
- What you do for God now will answer for you in times of need.
- Your seed holds the key to your future.

How Should You Give?

- The regular worship offering (2 Chronicles 6:29; Mark 12:41-44).
- Tithes (and first fruits) (Genesis 14:18-20; Malachi 3:10-11; Proverbs 3:9-10; Matthew 23:23).
- Kingdom project giving (Exodus 35:5-11; 1Chronicles 29:2-3; Ezra 6:14; Luke 7:2-6).
- Vows and sacrifices (1Samuel 1:11; Psalm 126:1-5, 132:1-5).
- Giving to the less privileged (Proverbs 19:17; Psalm 41:1).
- Responsibility giving – giving to wife, children, biological parents, spiritual parents, mentors, etc. (Ephesians 6:1-3; Galatians 6:6; Genesis 27:1-4).

Your giving is an investment that will surely be rewarded. Additionally, generous parents tend to raise generous children. Stinginess and greed in some people can be traced to their parents. Mike Murdock says, "Giving is the proof that you have conquered greed." Selfishness always diminishes what you have gained. Become a covenant giver!

How to Develop a Covenant Mentality

A **covenant mentality** means living with a deep awareness that you're in a binding, personal relationship with God – a relationship based on love, obedience, trust, and honor. Here's how to develop it:

1. Understand the Reliability of the Covenant

Deuteronomy 7:9 says,

> *"Know therefore that the Lord your God is God, the faithful God who keeps covenant and steadfast love with those who love him and keep his commandments, to a thousand generations."*

Be convinced about the infallibility, unchangeability, or trustworthiness of God's covenant promises. Friend, the covenant is reliable and the Covenant-Keeper is infallible. God cannot lie. He cannot change, nor can He fail you. Read the stories of people who lived covenant lives to boost your faith.

2. Respond to God's Call to a Covenant Life

Covenant starts with God's invitation. Just as He called Abraham (Nehemiah 9:7-8), God has called you into a relationship with Him. Romans 8:28 says those who love God are

> *"Called according to His purpose."*

You're not here by chance; you've been personally invited into God's covenant.

Like Abraham, enter the covenant by faith in the blood of Jesus Christ and be committed to living a life of obedience. Teach your family the same by your example.

3. Maintain the Covenant Daily

Like any relationship, a covenant requires attention and consistency. Jesus gave us the Holy Communion as a way to remember and renew our covenant with Him (1 Corinthians 11:24-25). Spend time with God, obey His Word, and live with covenant awareness. Go to the communion table frequently to renew your covenant. Be conscious that the covenant in the blood of Jesus Christ is superior to all other covenants that the devil may want to impose on you.

4. Love God, Not Just Follow Rituals

In Hosea 6:6, God says,

"I want you to show love, not offer sacrifices."

God wants a **relationship**, not empty religion. Unlike idols that impose fearful transactions, God wants your heart. Spend time with Him – pray, worship, fast, and let Him shape your life.

I noticed spiritual attacks came against my home when I traveled. So, I began holding family retreats before I left for my journeys. The enemy's power was broken over my household. When you seek God, His presence covers your home.

5. Honor God Deeply

"They greatly revered me and stood in awe of my name" (Malachi 2:5).

In this verse, God praised the priests from the family of Levi, who kept the covenant by honoring Him.

Child of God, begin to honor God more than you honor men. I see people spend millions honoring deceased parents with billboards, tombs, and sumptuous funerals. But how much do we honor **the Living God**? Show him your awe, love, and loyalty. He deserves your highest respect, not remains.

6. Be Faithful to the Covenant

"They did not remain faithful… so I turned my back on them" (Hebrews 8:9).

Covenant blessing flows from **faithfulness**. Stay loyal. Stay obedient. God never breaks His word; don't break yours. He will surely intervene and change your story. The devil cannot stop you in the covenant.

In Summary

We have seen that a covenant with God is not just a spiritual agreement; it's a life-altering relationship. When you live with a covenant mentality, you walk in divine protection, direction, and blessing, not just for yourself, but for your family and future generations. Choose to live with

God-only trust, God-first priorities, unshakable faith in His promises, and quick obedience to His voice. The covenant you honor today will shape the destiny of your family tomorrow. Live it. Teach it. Pass it on!

PRAYER POINTS
Thanksgiving:

1. *Father, thank You for inviting me into a covenant relationship with You, in Jesus' name.*
2. *Thank You, Lord, for being a Covenant-Keeper who never fails or lies, in Jesus' name.*
3. *Thank You, Father, for the blood of Jesus that brought me into the New Covenant, in Jesus' name.*
4. *Lord, I give You praise for the generational blessings that come through covenant obedience, in Jesus' name.*

Repentance and Consecration:

5. *Father, forgive me for claiming Your promises while ignoring Your requirements, in Jesus' name.*
6. *Lord, have mercy on me for every act of syncretism and idolatry in my life and family, in Jesus' name.*
7. *I repent of shallow commitment and delayed obedience, in Jesus' name.*
8. *Father, I break every ungodly covenant I've entered with the devil knowingly or unknowingly, in Jesus' name.*
9. *Father, cleanse me from all double-mindedness and spiritual compromise, in Jesus' name.*
10. *O Father, purify my heart and renew a steadfast spirit within me, in Jesus' name.*
11. *Lord, burn away the desire to trust in man or riches instead of You, in Jesus' name.*
12. *Father, I surrender fully to Your will and purposes for my life, in Jesus' name.*
13. *Let every idol hidden in my heart be uprooted by Your fire, in Jesus' name.*
14. *I dedicate my life afresh as a living sacrifice before You, in Jesus' name.*

Family Commitment to Worship and Service:

15. *Father, help me lead my family into a deeper covenant relationship with You, in Jesus' name.*
16. *Let our home be an altar of worship and obedience to You, in Jesus' name.*

17. *May every member of my family become a disciple of Jesus Christ, in Jesus' name.*

18. *Lord, ignite in us a desire to serve You wholeheartedly, in Jesus' name.*

19. *I declare that our family shall not serve idols or engage in religious hypocrisy, in Jesus' name.*

20. *May our family history be rewritten through a covenant walk with God, in Jesus' name.*

21. *I declare that our house shall be known for righteousness and truth, in Jesus' name.*

22. *Let our children inherit spiritual passion and covenant blessings, in Jesus' name.*

23. *Lord, use our family as a lighthouse to other families and communities, in Jesus' name.*

24. *May we serve God with our talents, time, and resources without reservation, in Jesus' name.*

Unity and Love in the Family:

25. *Father, bind our hearts together in love and unity, in Jesus' name.*

26. *Father, we reject every spirit of division, misunderstanding, and offense, in Jesus' name.*

27. *Father, teach us to forgive one another and walk in harmony, in Jesus' name.*

28. *Father, fill our hearts with genuine love that reflects Your heart, in Jesus' name.*

29. *Father, let every barrier to unity in our home be destroyed, in Jesus' name.*

30. *Father, make our family a reflection of heaven's love, in Jesus' name.*

31. *Father, heal every wound that is hindering love in our relationships, in Jesus' name.*

32. *Father, restore broken bonds and disconnected hearts in our family, in Jesus' name.*

33. *Father, we declare that selfishness will not have a place in our home, in Jesus' name.*

34. *Father, may our family be knitted together in love, patience, and mutual honor, in Jesus' name.*

Peace and Divine Order:

35. *Lord, establish Your peace over every storm in our family, in Jesus' name.*

36. *I declare divine order in every relationship and responsibility in this family, in Jesus' name.*

37. *Let confusion and chaos be replaced by godly wisdom and peace, in Jesus' name.*

38. *Father, let our family become a sanctuary of peace and refuge, in Jesus' name.*

39. *I reject every demonic assignment to bring disorder into our family, in Jesus' name.*

Prophetic Declarations and Covenant Mentality:

40. *I declare that our family walks under an open heaven, in Jesus' name.*

41. *We shall not lack any good thing as we walk in obedience, in Jesus' name.*

42. *We are blessed with every spiritual blessing in heavenly places, in Jesus' name.*

43. *The covenant of grace shall speak continually over our family, in Jesus' name.*

44. *We are covenant children, and no evil shall prevail over us, in Jesus' name.*

45. *Generational blessings are resting on our household, in Jesus' name.*

46. *We shall be known as a family that honors God above all else, in Jesus' name.*

Cameroon:

47. *We thank You for the Church in Cameroon and every believer standing in the gap, in Jesus' name.*

48. *Thank You for the resources, talents, and beauty You have blessed our land with, in Jesus' name.*

49. *We thank You because You are still on the throne and rule over the affairs of this nation, in Jesus' name.*

50. *Lord, cleanse the land from wicked altars and evil covenants established by leaders or ancestors, in Jesus' name.*

The Altar and the Word

"I am reminded of your sincere faith, a faith that dwelt first in your grandmother Lois and your mother Eunice and now, I am sure, dwells in you as well" (2 Timothy 1:5).

A strong family altar establishes God's presence in the home and sets the foundation for His lasting blessing upon the family. Writing in *Influence Magazine*, Samuel Rodriguez put it powerfully: *"Show me a family altar, and I will show a house where God's presence resides."* And where God's presence dwells, good things begin to happen. Hearts are healed, lives are restored, and destinies are shaped.

Is your family facing crisis, division, or spiritual stagnation? Do you long to see peace, unity, and God's blessing passed down to your children and grandchildren? Here is a powerful, time-tested truth: Establish a solid family altar.

The family altar is more than a tradition; it's a meeting place between heaven and earth, a space where your family comes under the covering of God's Word, worship, and prayer. It is a spiritual gate through which God's voice is heard, His guidance is received, and His blessings are released on your family.

Let me be clear: destroying evil altars is important, but it is not enough. Burning idols and tearing down shrines is only the beginning. If you want the heavens to open over your household, you must intentionally build and maintain a strong family altar. That is where revival and family restoration begin.

My Family Altar

The destiny of the Tangumonkem Family has been profoundly shaped by the power of prayer and the Word at our family altar.

I can't remember exactly when it all began, but I do know this: morning devotion was constant in our home. My parents surrendered their lives to Jesus Christ in the early 1970s and have remained fervent believers ever since. As I grew, I found myself worshipping with them in the Full Gospel Mission. What stood out to me most was their passion for living out God's Word. That profoundly influenced my understanding of Christianity. From their example, I learned that being a Christian means living fully for Jesus Christ.

Every morning, between 5:00 am and 5:30 am, either Dad or Mom would wake us for family devotion. We sang songs, read the Bible, and Dad, who usually led, would preach briefly, then lead us in a short time of prayer. This was a daily routine and became a core part of our upbringing.

Whether we liked it or not, we showed up. And we couldn't skip it. Dad and Mom had a no-excuse follow-up system. Many times, Dad's calm but firm voice, or Mom's sharp tone, would interrupt my early morning sweet dreams. "Oh, mom again with this her prayer thing!" I dragged myself to the sitting room. Most days, I walked to the sitting room half-asleep and grumbling, but those moments left a permanent mark on my life. I still remember them vividly.

Our learning wasn't limited to Scripture alone. Dad and Mom often used those times to share life lessons, drawing from personal experiences or stories they had heard. They taught us to fear God, respect others, avoid ungodly influences, and pursue excellence.

The family altar also served as a gathering place for the family, where major announcements were made. One early morning, Dad cleared his throat and announced, "We are going to start building our house soon." We received it with great excitement because we had never experienced it before.

It wasn't just about morning devotions either. Occasionally, Dad or Mom would declare a day of fasting. We didn't always welcome the announcement, but we were expected to join. At times, we went to church together to pray. Sometimes, they fasted without us, but we all knew our family was built around the altar.

When I Started My Family

The spiritual practices I learned at the family altar while growing up under my parents became the foundation for building my own family altar when I married Anna. Praying together came naturally to us. When we began having children, involving them in morning prayers became instinctive. As the bishop of my house, I simply applied what I had learned from growing up under my senior bishop, Pa Lekunze A.T.

Every morning, our children acted just as we did when we were kids. They would wrap themselves in blankets and wait for either my wife or me to call them for morning devotion. One morning, my six-year-old son Daniel asked his mother, "Mama, can't we rest at least a day from this early morning devotion?" She replied, "Oh no, Dan. God's altar needs fire every morning – we can't allow the fire to go out." Dan then dragged himself to the sitting room to join our daily family ritual.

As our children grew older and learned to read, we began assigning them to lead the devotions. Each family member eventually had a day to lead. For years now, Anna has led the family devotion every Monday morning, while I take Thursdays. The children lead on the remaining days. Whenever one of us is absent, we appoint another "Pastor" to stand in.

Over time, we have used various devotional guides to enrich our family altar moments. However, starting in 2011, we adopted the *Prayer Storm Daily Prayer Guide* as our family devotional. It has been a fantastic experience. We also observe family fasting days and occasionally organize family retreats.

One powerful lesson our children have learned from the family altar is that God answers prayers. On multiple occasions, we assign key prayer topics to each person, and after praying over time, we all come back with testimonies that God has answered. We've witnessed God move in dramatic ways. I recall when our building project got stuck, we called for a family fast on a Friday. We poured our hearts out to our Heavenly Father. Miraculously, fresh ideas came, and financial provision began to flow. We knew the burden had been lifted.

As we continue to pray together, God has also spoken to us through prophetic dreams and visions, offering insight and direction for the family and individual members. The family altar has not only united us spiritually but has become a sacred space where heaven's voice is heard and God's power revealed to us.

What Is a Family Altar?

In simple terms, a family altar is a dedicated time and space in the home where the entire family gathers to pray, worship, and study God's Word together. It is a sacred moment of shared intimacy with the Living God; a spiritual meeting point where heaven touches the home.

The family altar is not necessarily a physical structure made of stones or wood, like in the Old Testament, but rather a consistent practice of seeking God as a family. It can happen in a sitting room, a corner of the house, or even in a specially designated room. What matters most is not the place, but the heart and habit behind it.

In my family, we usually gather in the sitting room for our altar moments. However, I've also seen families go the extra mile to create physical spaces devoted to God. For example, when I visited the family compound of Governor Ivaha Dieudonné, I was deeply moved to find a beautiful chapel built right on the property – a sanctuary dedicated to the Lord.

Whether humble or grand, every home needs an altar. It is the spiritual firewall of the family, a protective barrier that resists Satan's schemes and draws down the peace, power, and presence of God.

The saying is true: *"The family that prays together, stays together."* If you show me a family that gathers at the altar, I will show you a house where God's presence rests and His power is at work. The family altar shapes destinies, heals broken relationships, guides decisions, and imparts strength during hard seasons. It's where children learn to fear the Lord and where spouses align their hearts with God and each other.

Never underestimate the impact of this simple yet powerful discipline. Your family altar can alter the life of your family for good.

Not a Physical Altar!

A family altar is **not** a structure made of stone or wood. It is a spiritual discipline that grounds your family in God's truth, love, and purpose.

Due to past exposure to idolatry, some believers struggle to worship the Living God without physical objects. As a result, they attempt to create altars using candles, incense, special anointing oils, stones, and so-called "Anointed items." In one book written by a pastor based in Bamenda, Cameroon, readers are instructed to use colored candles and crucifixes to construct altars and pray at midnight. These practices may appear spiritual, but can dangerously open doors to demonic forces.

You must understand that altars function as spiritual gateways connecting the physical and spiritual realms. Jesus clearly said, *"I am the door"* (John 10:9). He is the only legal access to the realm of the Living God. Any other "Spiritual gate" is unauthorized and can be a gateway into darkness. Therefore, be vigilant against the dangers of syncretism and deceptive "anointed objects."

A woman once came to us for deliverance after strange spiritual attacks began in her home. A false prophet had built an altar there using various candles and mystical objects. What she thought would invite God's presence instead invited bondage.

As New Testament believers, we are not instructed to build physical altars. There is no single New Testament scripture commanding this practice. Neither Apostle Paul nor any of the Early Church fathers built physical altars. The only physical element Jesus commanded for worship is the Holy Communion. Anything beyond that becomes a dangerous distraction from Christ.

In Exodus 20:22-23, God warned Israel against mixing worship with objects:

> ***"You have seen for yourselves that I have spoken to you from heaven: Do not make any gods to be alongside me; do not make for yourselves gods of silver or gods of gold."***

A family altar is a spiritual gathering where family members seek God together. It is not a mini-shrine with religious objects. If you've gathered items from various sources to build an altar in your home, it's time to let them go. Let Christ alone be the center of your worship.

The Family Altar: A Foundation Stone for Family Blessings

One of the most powerful yet often neglected keys to unlocking God's blessing in the home is the family altar.

Throughout Scripture, those who built altars to God experienced His favor and passed down generational blessings. Abraham regularly built altars as acts of family worship (Genesis 12:7-8; 13:18). In Genesis 18:19, God said this about him:

"I have chosen him so he may command his children... to keep the way of the Lord."

His obedience and commitment to walk in God's ways laid the foundation for a blessed lineage.

Joshua was another person whose family altar had a profound impact on his family. He declared,

"As for me and my house, we will serve the Lord" (Joshua 24:15).

He modeled covenant leadership that influenced his entire household.

Cornelius is a New Testament example of a man whose family altar impacted his household and community. In Acts 10, we are told he was

"A devout man who feared God with all his household."

His family altar of prayer led to salvation for his entire household. His family became the first Gentiles to experience the baptism of the Holy Spirit. Surely, several persons were brought into the Kingdom through them. Do you see how your family altar can attract God's power and make you agents of revival and restoration?

1. The Place of Fellowship And Intimacy With Our God

It is where we interact with Him and know Him personally, not just ask things from Him. Through our communication, we deepen our relationship with God. Individuals and families without active prayer altars have a very shallow knowledge of God.

2. The Place of Consecration

Our sins are exposed and expelled by the blood of Jesus Christ at the prayer altar. We learn from Isaiah 6:1-7 that when you see the Almighty God, you see your iniquity. In the light of His Holiness, your filthiness is exposed. That is why praying men and women are holy people. You cannot live in His presence and enjoy sin. Look at the lives of Jeremiah, Samuel, Paul the Apostle, and Queen Esther. They were prayerful and holy people.

3. The Place of Revival

We experience personal and generational revival at the prayer altar. Elijah prayed on Mount Carmel with all his heart, and revival broke out (1 Kings 18). Evan Roberts prayed for 13 years for revival in Wales, and it came. William J. Seymour prayed for 5 and a half hours for 5 years and two more years, 7 and a half hours, and the Azusa Street revival came. We fan the flames of the Holy Ghost when we pray in the Spirit (2 Timothy 1:6).

4. The Place of Planting The Seed of God's Word

The family altar is a place where the children receive the seed of God's Word. At the family altar, Abraham commanded his children to walk in God's ways (Genesis 18:19). Doesn't it amaze you that his offspring did not disconnect from God? Isaac, Jacob, Joseph, and their children's children loved the God of their ancestor, Abraham.

Today, how many of our children who grew up in the Church with us continue to serve God as adults? Several church kids end up wayward, far from God. Why? The parents have part of the blame. They fail to command them to keep the way of the Lord, like Abraham did.

The Hebrew word translated as "Command" in Genesis 18:19 means "Giving instructions, orders, or directives with authority." This implies that Abraham taught his children God's ways, commandments, and statutes. He led his household in worship and modeled the faith to them through his obedience and worship. He kept the covenant before them and also taught them how to keep it.

In Deuteronomy 6:6-9, God instructs us on how to instill the Word in our children:

"These words, which I am commanding you today, shall be [written] on your heart and mind. You shall teach them diligently to your [a]children [impressing God's precepts on their minds and penetrating their hearts with His truths] and shall speak of them when you sit in your house and when you walk on the road and when you lie down and when you get up. And you shall bind them as a sign on your hand (forearm), and they shall be used as [b]bands (frontals, frontlets) on your forehead. You shall write them on the [c]doorposts of your house and on your gates" (Deuteronomy 6:6-9 AMP).

As parents, we are supposed to teach diligently, earnestly, frequently, and discreetly. This can only be done by parents who are wholeheartedly committed to seeing their children grow in God's ways. Sadly, many Christian parents are not true role models to their children. How do you expect them to become true disciples of Christ when all they see in you is hypocrisy? We are told that children copy what they see you doing more than what you ask them to do. As I mentioned earlier, I replicate the things I saw my parents doing on my family altar today. In contrast, some couples struggle to cultivate the habit of praying with their children every day because their parents did not train them. Anna and I do it with great ease because we were both raised in homes where the family altar was practiced daily.

Let your family altar become a place where you intentionally plant the seed of God's Word in your family members. Pastor Tony Evans once said, *"The single most powerful tool for shaping a child's future is a family altar."* Unfortunately, if we don't train our children to serve God, Satan will make them his servants.

Timothy, a Perfect Example
Paul wrote this about Timothy:

"I am reminded of your sincere faith, which first lived in your grandmother Lois and in your mother Eunice and, I am persuaded, now lives in you also" (2 Timothy 1:5).

Timothy was the son of a Jewish-Christian mother, Eunice, and a Greek father (Acts 16:1). Though his father was likely not a believer, Timothy was raised in a godly home shaped by his mother and grandmother. These women are commended for passing on a sincere, active faith that profoundly shaped Timothy's spiritual growth.

From childhood, Timothy received the seed of Christian faith from his mother. Simply put, he came to Christ through her. How many Christian parents today can say their children have become genuine disciples through their influence? Sadly, some children reject the Gospel because of the hypocrisy they see in their parents.

In an era when women had limited public influence in religion, Eunice and Lois played a pivotal role in shaping the future of a church leader. Their teaching, rooted in the Hebrew Scriptures and fulfilled in Christ, laid the foundation for Timothy's life and ministry.

We must be intentional about discipling our children:

First, by living authentic Christian lives before them.

Second, by teaching them the Gospel with clarity.

Third, by showing Christlike love, firm yet unconditional.

5. The Place of Security

The family altar invites God's presence, and where His presence dwells, His blessings flow. Proverbs 3:33 says,

"The Lord blesses the home of the righteous" (Proverbs 3:33).

In a world filled with moral confusion, cultural distractions, and destructive satanic activities, your altar becomes a **spiritual defense system for the security of your family.**

"He that dwelleth in the secret place of the most High shall abide under the shadow of the Almighty" (Psalm 91:1 KJV).

Do you want your family to enjoy supernatural protection? Establish a family altar. Most families that do not have a prayer altar end up turning to agents of the devil for protection. A praying home becomes a blessed home, where God leads, provides, and protects across generations.

Some time ago, while I was studying in Togo, I had a dream in which the enemy was attacking my son. Alarmed, I asked my classmates to join me in prayer for the protection of my family. Later, I called home, and my wife told me that our son had come to her room at midnight, saying, "I'm going to die." Thank God, she quickly discerned it was a demonic attack and began rebuking the devil, commanding him to release the child. The cloud of darkness lifted, and he began to explain what had happened that day at school. A group of boys—his classmates—had gathered behind their classroom and sent one of them to fetch him. At first, he refused, but after pressure, he went. They surrounded him, and one boy placed a hand on his head, beginning to chant. A dark cloud fell over him immediately. Sadly, he didn't tell his mother after school until the demon of death came for him at night. Imagine what could have happened if my wife didn't know how to pray. How many children have been spiritually attacked and even destroyed in school because they had no one covering them in prayer?

Your family altar is your place of spiritual power and protection—don't neglect it.

6. The Family Altar Strengthens Unity

The saying is true: "A family that prays together stays together." A consistent life of prayer at the family altar not only invites God's presence but also builds unity, deepens trust, and strengthens emotional bonds within the home.

A University of Notre Dame study found that families who engage in regular religious practices, especially prayer, report higher levels of emotional closeness and relational satisfaction. Similarly, Barna Research reveals that teens who pray with their families are more likely to stay in the faith and maintain strong relationships with their parents.[2] Hence, one of the greatest gifts you can give your household is the daily habit of praying together.

For married couples, prayer brings a powerful connection. It softens hearts, breaks pride, and aligns both spouses with God's will. As Stormie Omartian wrote, *"Prayer is intimacy with God, but when done together, it becomes intimacy with one another as well."*

Biblical examples affirm this truth. Abraham and Sarah built altars together, passing a legacy of faith to Isaac and Jacob (Genesis 12:7-

8; 18:19). Mary and Joseph stayed united through divine challenges by trusting God together in prayer.

A survey by the National Association of Marriage Enhancement found that less than 1% of couples who pray together daily divorce.[3] One couple on the brink of separation began praying silently together each morning. That silence turned to confession, forgiveness, and healing. Within months, their marriage was restored, not just by counseling, but through the power of prayer.

Your family altar should be more than a tradition. Let it be a place where hearts unite, wounds heal, and love deepens. In a world full of conflict and distraction, let your family altar anchor your home in peace, presence, and unity.

7. A Prophetic Launchpad for Destiny

The family prayer altar is more than a place of devotion; it is a prophetic launchpad where destinies are activated, directed, and protected. It is at the altar that God releases guidance, blessings, and covering over every member of the household.

Jacob received the patriarchal blessing at his family altar before leaving home (Genesis 28:1-4). Though he fled in fear, God's presence followed him. At Bethel, he encountered the Lord in a dream, confirming the blessing and guiding him to his uncle Laban. Years later, that same presence led him back to the Promised Land, fulfilling his divine destiny.

In contrast, many lives are derailed because they are shaped not by God's altar, but by evil altars – sources of manipulation, bondage, and confusion. Children from homes with holy altars thrive because their paths are aligned with God's will. Those raised under evil altars often suffer spiritual oppression, stagnation, and cycles of failure. As Dr. Paul Enenche says, *"Where there is no prayer fire in the home, strange fires will rise."*

Studies affirm the positive impact of family altars on the destinies of children. According to Barna Research, youth from families that engage in regular prayer and worship are more likely to pursue purpose-driven lives, make wiser decisions, and maintain long-term faith.[4] Do you want your children and family members to walk in their divine destinies? Connect them to God's altar. Let your family altar become a place where purpose is declared, identity is shaped, and lives are launched into God's promises.

Steps to Develop Your Family Altar

Establishing a family altar doesn't require the perfect setting, the longest prayer, or a seminary degree. What matters most is consistency, sincerity, and unity.

> *"The fire shall ever be burning upon the altar; it shall never go out" (Leviticus 6:13 KJV).*

Here are five simple and practical steps to help you develop your family altar:

1. Set a Consistent Time

Proverbs 8:34 says, *"Blessed is the man who listens to me, watching daily at my doors..."*

Choose a time that works well for your family—morning or evening. Consistency builds habits, and habits build a legacy.

In our home, we meet every morning at 5:30 a.m. for family prayer. Saturdays and Sundays are set aside for individual personal prayer. Select a pattern that meets your family's needs.

2. Read the Word Together

Psalm 119:105 says,

> *"Your word is a lamp to my feet and a light to my path."*

Read a short Bible passage together, around 5 to 10 verses. Let each person take turns reading aloud. This encourages engagement and spiritual growth in everyone. You can also use a family devotional guide. In our home, we use the *Prayer Storm Daily Prayer Guide*.

Occasionally, we read inspirational Christian books as a family. Whatever you do, make time for God's Word daily. Provide Bibles for your family members.

3. Discuss the Passage

Deuteronomy 6:7 says,

> *"Teach them diligently to your children..."*

After reading, ask questions like, "What does this passage mean?" or "How can we live this today?" Allow the children to speak too—their insights are often profound.

Every Sunday at 8:00 p.m., we have a family Bible study using the Discovering God's Love (DGL) model. After reading, we answer four questions:

1) What is God saying to you in this passage?
2) What does this passage reveal about God?
3) How will you apply this in your life?
4) Who will you share God's love with in the next 48 hours?

This simple format has become a tremendous blessing to our family, drawing us closer to God and one another. Nothing unites people like God's Word and prayer.

4. Pray as a Family

Matthew 18:20 says,

> *"Where two or three gather in my name, there am I with them."*

Pray together for your needs, concerns, and blessings. Let everyone take turns praying, including the children. Give each person a prayer focus. For example, Dad prays for the family's health, Mom prays for finances, and a child prays for school or friends. This builds responsibility and spiritual sensitivity.

In our family, we rotate leadership of the prayer time, with each person taking a turn leading the devotion. We also schedule family fasts when necessary, joining our hearts to seek God's intervention and blessing.

5. Develop an Altar for Your Extended Family

Judges 6:25-26 says,

> *"...pull down the altar of Baal that your father has, and cut down the Asherah that is beside it and build an altar to the Lord your God..."*

After you've established a regular altar in your household, consider building a spiritual altar with your extended family – siblings, cousins, and relatives. Encourage them to come together and seek God corporately.

In Judges, God told Gideon to destroy the evil altar in his father's house before building a holy altar to the Lord. Many family struggles today are rooted in generational issues that require a corporate altar of prayer and repentance to deal with.

In our extended family, we meet twice a year – once physically, and once online. Family members outside the country join virtually. These meetings have brought tremendous breakthroughs, healing, and spiritual restoration in our family.

You can meet weekly, monthly, or yearly – whatever works best for you. The key is intentionality and consistency. If needed, invite trusted spiritual leaders to help you lead such gatherings, especially if your family is facing spiritual battles you feel unequipped to handle alone.

Raise Your Altar

Now that you understand the vital role of the altar in releasing God's blessings on your family, what will you do about it? The best place to begin is with your personal altar. Apply the lessons you've learned, then bring your immediate family together, and eventually your extended family. John L. Mason said, *"The strongest action you can take in any situation is to go to your knees and ask God for help."*

God's power will no longer be absent in your home. Evil spiritual forces will be crushed under your feet. Your loved ones will begin to rise into places you never imagined. The family altar will release a fresh anointing of restoration over your household. Raise your altar!

You don't need to be perfect; just be consistent. Let your house become a dwelling place for God's glory.

PRAYER POINTS
Thanksgiving:

1. *Father, thank You for the gift of salvation and the privilege to build an altar in our home, in Jesus' name.*
2. *Lord, we thank You for every seed of truth and righteousness planted in our family through Your Word, in Jesus' name.*
3. *Thank You, Lord, for the legacy of faith passed down by our spiritual and biological parents, in Jesus' name.*
4. *Father, we thank You for the times You have spoken to our family through the altar, guiding and preserving us, in Jesus' name.*

Repentance and Consecration:

5. *Father, forgive us for neglecting our family altar and prioritizing worldly things over Your presence, in Jesus' name.*

6. *Father, cleanse us from every spiritual laziness, hypocrisy, and double life, in Jesus' name.*

7. *Father, we repent of every compromise that has opened doors to darkness in our family, in Jesus' name.*

8. *Let the blood of Jesus cleanse our altar and restore its purity and power, in Jesus' name.*

9. *Father, purify our hearts so we may offer true worship and obedience as a family, in Jesus' name.*

10. *Father, consecrate our family members to You afresh; set us apart for Your glory, in Jesus' name.*

Commitment to Worship and the Word:

11. *Father, help us establish a consistent family altar that honors You daily, in Jesus' name.*

12. *Father, let our hearts burn with a fresh desire to worship and seek You as a family, in Jesus' name.*

13. *Father, may our home be a sanctuary where Your Word is honored and obeyed, in Jesus' name.*

14. *Father, give us grace to train our children in Your ways and model true faith before them, in Jesus' name.*

15. *Father, let our moments of devotion be filled with Your presence and power, in Jesus' name.*

16. *Father, let Your Word be planted deeply in the hearts of our children through the altar, in Jesus' name.*

Family Discipleship and Spiritual Growth:

17. *Lord, let every member of our family become a passionate disciple of Jesus Christ, in Jesus' name.*

18. *We declare that our children will grow up to love, serve, and obey You all their lives, in Jesus' name.*

19. *Father, let our home become a training ground for raising kingdom ambassadors, in Jesus' name.*

20. *Lord, let every lesson taught at our family altar shape godly character in our children, in Jesus' name.*

21. *Father, let the truth of the Gospel take deep root in the hearts of our entire household, in Jesus' name.*
22. *We commit to making Your Word the foundation of all we do as a family, in Jesus' name.*

Protection and Security:

23. *Father, let Your presence become a shield around our family because of the altar, in Jesus' name.*
24. *Father, let the fire on our altar become a wall of protection against every demonic invasion, in Jesus' name.*
25. *Lord, protect our children from evil altars, spiritual traps, and ungodly influences, in Jesus' name.*
26. *Let every demonic plan assigned against our family be aborted by the power of our family altar, in Jesus' name.*
27. *May we always abide under the shadow of the Almighty through our consistent fellowship, in Jesus' name.*

Unity, Love, and Intimacy in the Family:

28. *Lord, use our family altar to heal broken relationships and restore unity in our family, in Jesus' name.*
29. *Father, let every spirit of offense, bitterness, and misunderstanding be routed out at our altar, in Jesus' name.*
30. *Father, we declare that our home shall be filled with love, understanding, and mutual respect, in Jesus' name.*
31. *Father, strengthen our marriage and let prayer draw us closer together as husband and wife, in Jesus' name.*
32. *May the atmosphere in our home reflect the peace and joy of the Holy Spirit, in Jesus' name.*

Revelation, Direction, and Prophetic Insight:

33. *Father, open our ears to hear Your voice clearly whenever we meet at the altar, in Jesus' name.*
34. *Father, release dreams, visions, and divine insight to guide our family, in Jesus' name.*
35. *Father, let our altar become a prophetic gateway to discern Your will and plans, in Jesus' name.*
36. *Father, may every decision we take as a family be birthed in prayer and revelation, in Jesus' name.*

37. *Father, silence every strange voice that contradicts Your Word in our home, in Jesus' name.*
38. *Father, give us direction for our future, education, careers, and assignments through the family altar, in Jesus' name.*

Prophetic Declarations:

39. *We declare that our family altar will activate generational blessings, in Jesus' name.*
40. *Like Abraham, I will pass down a heritage of faith and righteousness, in Jesus' name.*
41. *Our children shall not depart from the Lord but shall walk in His truth always, in Jesus' name.*
42. *The fire on our altar will never go out, but will burn from one generation to another, in Jesus' name.*
43. *Our family altar will become a memorial to the faithfulness of God, in Jesus' name.*
44. *Our home shall be known as a dwelling place for the presence of God, in Jesus' name.*
45. *As for me and my house, we shall serve the Lord, and walk in His ways forever, in Jesus' name.*

Cameroon

46. *Father, thank You for the peace we've enjoyed thus far, despite tensions and unrest, in Jesus' name.*
47. *Father, have mercy on our nation for every form of injustice, corruption, and bloodshed, in Jesus' name.*
48. *We repent for idolatry, tribalism, hatred, and shedding of innocent blood, in Jesus' name.*
49. *Father, frustrate every plot to cause violence, bloodshed, or civil war, in Jesus' name.*
50. *Let every plan to rig, destabilize, or manipulate the elections be exposed and fail, in Jesus' name.*

Chapter 3

Days 7-9

Obedience to Divine Instructions

"By faith Abraham obeyed when he was called to go out to a place that he was to receive as an inheritance. And he went out, not knowing where he was going (Hebrews 11:8).

Divine blessings travel in the direction of the obedient. There is no actual progress with God without complete submission to prophetic direction. Supernatural increase only comes through strict obedience to divine instructions. Kingdom prosperity comes through alignment with God's principles. Prayer and fasting for a whole year will not bring you prosperity; prosperity answers to your obedience to divine commandments.

Also, you cannot grow spiritually unless you are rooted in doing His Word. Your submission to God's commands will put you in command. Show me someone committed to obedience, and I'll show you someone rising to prominence.

Obedience builds a family; disobedience ruins it. Friend, any time you disobey divine instructions, you either stagnate or deviate from God's plan for your life, and in doing so, you hinder your family's destiny. Ask King Saul. He started by disobeying a simple instruction from the prophet Samuel:

> *"Then go down before me to Gilgal. And behold, I am coming down to you to offer burnt offerings and to sacrifice peace offerings. Seven days you shall wait, until I come to you and show you what you shall do" (1 Samuel 10:8).*

He waited for seven days, and Samuel did not come. Instead of either persevering or consulting God on what to do, he went on and offered the sacrifice. He was not supposed to do it because he wasn't a priest. Later, he defied God's command to eradicate the Amalekites (1 Samuel 15). His disobedience cost him enormously. He lost the kingdom, his children, and his life. His family never prospered in Israel.

Achan perished with his entire household because he disobeyed Joshua's command not to touch the spoils of the battle of Jericho (See Joshua 7). Disobedience always opens the door to destruction, no matter how small it may seem.

Friend, your obedience is crucial to receiving divine revelation and walking in God's blessings. Satan, being aware of this, wants you to disobey God and stray from His best plans for your life, then turn around and blame Him for abandoning you. How many are bitter against God because of the predicaments, after having wasted their God-given opportunities through rebellion?

What Am I Here For?

One of the greatest lessons God has taught me is this: your life assignment is often unlocked by asking the right questions. Discovering purpose begins with curiosity. Many people go through life frustrated, not because they lack potential, but because they never pause to ask the critical questions that point them toward their true purpose. It was by asking deep, intentional questions that I came to understand what I was created for. And this has brought profound peace to my soul. The ignorance of your life's purpose produces confusion, fear, and instability in your soul.

Often, divine direction comes to those who are teachable. Imagine someone traveling to an unknown destination but refusing to ask for directions. How likely is he to arrive safely or on time? The same is true of your calling and that of your family. If you don't seek clarity through the right questions, you may wander aimlessly and miss your life's purpose. You can't afford to waste your destiny by running the race of life without a road map. Thomas Carlyle rightly said, *"The man without a purpose is like a ship without a rudder, a waif, a nothing, a no man."*

Knowing your purpose or God's will for your life is the first step; pursuing it is the second and crucial step. Most people know what God wants, but are not willing to yield. This is rebellion! One day, while I was praying with a group of Christians for the baptism of the Holy Spirit. One of the members sat there distracted, showing no interest in what we were doing. Taken aback, I walked to her. "Sister, why are you not praying with us to be baptized by the Holy Spirit?" I asked. "I don't want to be filled with the Holy Spirit because He will ask me to do what I don't want," she responded bluntly. This, sadly, is the mindset of some Christians. They don't want to be led by God. A few weeks later, I was informed that she was admitted to the intensive care unit of the hospital. Unfortunately, I couldn't talk to her till she died. Rumors said she died because she was attempting to commit an abortion.

Friend, the best God has for you is in His will. You cannot get it elsewhere. No doubt, Jesus prayed for strength to do His Father's will until His sweat was mixed with blood (Luke 22:44). How passionate are you about knowing and doing God's will? Your future, or that of your family, is not guaranteed without God in your plan. Robert William states, *"Nothing matters more than knowing God's purposes for your life, and nothing can compensate for not knowing them."*

God Orders The Steps of The Righteous

God is committed to guiding His children meticulously through the various stages of life. This is because the path of life leads through defying dark tunnels, deep valleys, and high mountains. Without divine assistance, you can't fulfill your destiny.

The problem is that most of us devise our plans, then try to manipulate God to support us in accomplishing them. Since God cannot follow us in the wrong direction, many go alone and end up in frustration. No matter how fast you run in the wrong direction, you will never arrive at the right destination. If you want to escape disaster and regret, stick to

God's plan and will for your life. Ensure that you secure divine approval before you make any key decision concerning your life and family.

You may ask me, "Pastor, can I know God's will concerning my life with clarity?" The answer is YES! However, you must seek His counsel. Divine guidance is only guaranteed for sincere seekers.

He said, "Don't go now!"

I had been fasting for three days and praying alone in the church hall for hours daily, but I didn't hear a word from the Lord. When I returned home in the evening of the last day to break my fast, suddenly the Holy Spirit began to speak to me. I knelt in front of my bed and heard these words loud and clear: "Don't go to Mbalmayo for the degree course now; when the time comes, I will let you know." I felt disappointed, but I decided to submit to His will because I knew it was best for me.

I graduated from the Full Gospel Bible Institute (FGBI) with a Diploma in Theology and Pastoral Ministry in June 1996. One year later, in 1997, the degree program of West African Advanced School of Theology (WAAST) – Mbalmayo Extension Center was launched. I sat for the entrance exam and succeeded by God's grace. The founding director of the school, Rev. Jim Lemons, sent me a mail congratulating me for scoring 98% in the exam and inviting me to start the program. I received the mail with great excitement because I had a dream to further my studies, and here was the opportunity. Unfortunately, my joy turned sour because I didn't have the money to travel to Mbalmayo, nor did I have a sponsor to back me up. I eventually lost the opportunity.

The truth is that I had not prayed to find out whether it was God's will and the right time for me to pursue a degree course. Divine timing is crucial for getting God's best.

"He has made everything beautiful in its time" (Ecclesiastes 3:11).

Four years later, in 2002, somebody opted to provide part of the cost of my studies in Mbalmayo. This time, I decided to seek God's perfect will about the program before receiving the support. That is what led me to fast and pray for three days. Thank God for inspiring me to do so, and for the answer He gave me.

When the Holy Spirit told me not to go, I informed the sponsor that it was not yet God's time. The truth is that it was not easy for me because some of those who had graduated after me from the diploma program had already obtained their Bachelor's Degrees. From a human perspective, I felt like I had been left behind. Life is not supposed to be a competition with others. You must follow the plan God has designed for you strictly, which is different from the one He has for others.

In the year 2005, God spoke to me clearly that it was time to start the degree program. Miraculously, He provided all the finances I needed for the program. I was able to study through the Bachelor's Degree and Master's levels without stress. I spent millions of CFA francs on my studies with ease. Presently, I am preparing to start the doctoral program. Over time, I discovered that most of those I thought had left me behind did not have the opportunity to pursue a degree beyond the Bachelor's level.

It is crucial to follow God's plan one step at a time.

Why Am I Here?

At a critical moment in my life, I began earnestly seeking God for answers to some of life's most profound questions – questions about my purpose and destiny. I needed clarity. I wanted to know exactly where God wanted me to settle and how He intended for me to fulfill the ministry He had entrusted to me.

My spiritual hunger deepened as I studied the life of Adam. In Genesis 2:15, I encountered a powerful truth: after creating Adam, God gave him both a specific place and a clear assignment. It dawned on me that "Callings are tied to locations." I realized then that discovering my God-ordained place and purpose was not optional; it was essential. So, I began to pray: "Father, there are five continents in the world. I surrender my future to You. I am willing to go anywhere You choose – whether that's joining my two brothers in America or relocating to any other nation of Your choosing. I want to be where You want me to be." I was sincere. I was ready to do whatever God required of me.

Even though I was already faithfully serving as a pastor with the Full Gospel Mission Cameroon, I couldn't ignore the deep restlessness inside me. I knew, beyond doubt, that there was more. I told the Lord, with all honesty, that I was ready to obey Him no matter the cost, no matter how difficult or uncomfortable, if it meant living out the assignment He had designed for me. I even vowed to relocate to any part of the world, as long as it was in alignment with His will.

For nearly five years, I prayed, fasted, and pursued God with longing and intensity. In 2009, I set aside a week to fast away from home, drinking only milk and water. During that fast, God spoke clearly to me: ***"Your assignment is to labor for the revival and restoration of My people in Cameroon. Relocate to Yaoundé and serve Me there."*** That is why I am in Yaounde and not in Europe or America.

Many have asked why I didn't settle in Europe or the U.S., even after God opened doors to me to those nations. I recall an incident at Baltimore Airport following a trip to Chicago. A Senegalese woman, traveling with her children, asked where I was from. When I told her I had come from Cameroon for a short visit, she exclaimed in disbelief: "Do you mean you're going back to Africa? For what?" I told her I love Cameroon and I can't remain in the United States. I know where God has assigned me. I am certain. Why should I relocate to Germany, France, or the U.S. just because the opportunity is there? Has God sent me there?

Initially, my wife didn't fully embrace the idea of moving to Yaoundé. It wasn't until June 2013 – four years later that she clearly understood what God was saying. Once she aligned with the vision, we formally requested permission from our church leadership, Full Gospel Mission Cameroon, to be released from our pastoral duties so we could move as God had instructed. It took the church two years to evaluate the situation. Finally, in 2015, the General Superintendent officially released us to fulfill the assignment God had given us in Yaoundé.

We moved on September 12, 2015, and settled in Biyem-Assi, Yaounde. Some colleagues tried to discourage us. Others warned that we wouldn't survive without a local church to support us. But because it was God who sent us, we have seen His faithfulness. Ten years have passed, and He has blessed the ministry in our hands abundantly.

In 2016, just before the Anglophone crisis began, I had a vision. The *Prayer Storm Daily Prayer Guide*, which we had been publishing since 2011, began to spread from Yaoundé to various regions across Cameroon and beyond. Until then, we printed the prayer guide in Bamenda and distributed it from there. After the vision, I realized we had to relocate our printing operations to Yaoundé. It was a risky decision, but it was divinely inspired. Shortly after we moved, the Anglophone crisis erupted. Had we remained in Bamenda, our ministry, the Christian Restoration Network (CRN), might have been paralyzed.

Can you imagine what would have happened if I had gone my own way instead of seeking and submitting to God's will? My failure or stagnation would not have affected me alone; it would have affected my entire family. My prayer for you is that you will never take a single step out of God's plan for your life.

What Does It Mean To Obey God?
What Is Obedience?
Obedience is simply doing what God says. As Mary said in John 2:5,
> *"Whatever He tells you, do it."*

It means responding promptly to God's instructions and moving when He says move. True obedience is absolute surrender to God's will – following Him wholeheartedly, even when it doesn't make sense. For example, a key difference between a sheep and a goat is obedience. Sheep follow the shepherd; goats do not.

Jesus Christ And Obedience
Jesus is the ultimate model of obedience. His life demonstrates how obedience to God leads to the fulfillment of one's purpose and unlocks divine blessings – not just for him, but for all who follow his example.

Jesus obeyed the Father completely. John 6:38 says,
> *"For I have come down from heaven not to do my will but to do the will of him who sent me."*

Throughout the Gospels, you notice that Jesus' life and ministry were centered on obedience to His Father's will. His mission to save humanity depended on His unwavering submission to the Father, even when it involved suffering.

Jesus obeyed through suffering. Hebrews 5:8 says,

"Though He was a Son, yet He learned obedience by the things which He suffered."

Obedience wasn't easy for Jesus. Remember what He faced at Gethsemane. He prayed,

"Father, if you are willing, take this cup from me; yet not my will, but Yours be done" (Luke 22:42).

He chose obedience even when it meant going to the cross. Philippians 2:8 says,

"And being found in appearance as a man, He humbled Himself by becoming

obedient to death–even the death on the cross."

Jesus' obedience brought salvation to the world. His obedience led to the fulfillment of God's redemptive plan. Through His sacrificial death and resurrection, all who believe in Him receive eternal life.

Because of His obedience, God exalted Him above all. Likewise, if we want divine elevation, we must walk in obedience. Friend, God will use you to impact your family and this generation if you are consumed with a fervent desire to obey Him. If you are willing to follow His instructions even when it hurts.

The Human Heart is Rebellious

By nature, the human heart tends to resist God. Scripture describes it as

"Deceitful above all things, and desperately wicked" (Jeremiah 17:9).

This "Heart" represents our will, desires, and attitudes, often characterized by pride, selfishness, and resistance to change. People generally prefer to do things their own way, even when it opposes God's will. How often do you seek God's opinion before you make important decisions? Do you easily humble yourself and repent when God's Word exposes your sins?

God Himself laments this hardness and promises a solution:

"I will remove the heart of stone and give you a heart of flesh" (Ezekiel 36:26).

You can bring your heart to Him for a deep transformation. You open yourself up to God's transforming power every time you sincerely admit your sin and begin to ask for forgiveness and cleansing through the blood of Jesus Christ.

Disobedience Is a Spirit

Disobedience isn't just a choice, it's a spiritual influence. Ephesians 2:2 describes it as

"The spirit now at work in the sons of disobedience."

Satan uses this spirit to turn people away from God, knowing that disobedience brings divine judgment (Deuteronomy 27-28). People knowingly violate God's commands, fully aware of the consequences. Why? Because they are under the influence of the spirit of disobedience.

Unfortunately, when you are under the influence of the spirit of rebellion, you cannot free yourself through willpower alone. You need Jesus Christ to set you free. If you do nothing about breaking the yoke of rebellion over your soul, it's possible to be active in church and still be a "Son or daughter of disobedience."

Why You Need the Spirit of Obedience

Obedience is also a spirit. In Acts 5:32, the Holy Spirit is described as the Spirit of obedience. He empowers us to obey God.

Here is why you need to be ruled by the Spirit of obedience:

1) To defeat the spirit of disobedience: Only the Spirit of obedience can conquer the influence of rebellion in your life and the lives of your family members.

2) To obey challenging instructions: God's commands can be very difficult sometimes, even illogical. Yet, obedience brings miracles. Abraham was told to relocate at 75 and later asked to offer his son; acts that only make sense to a heart empowered by obedience.

3) To experience divine promotion: Obedience leads to progress; disobedience leads to loss. Saul lost his throne due to disobedience, while David rose through humble obedience.

4) To Operate in Spiritual Authority: When we submit to God, we gain authority over evil. James 4:7 says,

"Submit to God. Resist the devil, and he will flee."

Evil spirits obey those who obey God (2 Corinthians 10:6). You cannot command them when you live in disobedience to authority. Saint Augustine said, "Disobedience turned angels to devils." Disobedience identifies you with devils and causes them to despise your authority.

5) To grow closer to God: Intimacy with God is directly tied to obedience.

"You are My friends if you do whatever I command you" (John 15:14).

You can't walk in God's presence in disobedience.

Often, our biggest challenge is not hearing God's voice, but obeying it. That's why God has promised to give us a new heart and a new spirit:

"I will put My Spirit within you and cause you to walk in My statutes" (Ezekiel 36:26-27).

Ask God, in faith, to baptize you with the Spirit of obedience. As you grow in obedience, you will walk in greater favor, power, and intimacy with God.

Dimensions of Obedience

Obedience to God is more than just compliance; it is a heart posture of trust, reverence, and alignment with His will.

1. To Walk Before Him

To obey God means to walk before Him in integrity, faithfulness, and reverence. This implies living with the consciousness that God is always watching and leading. It's about daily choices that reflect your devotion and commitment to Him. It also means living transparently, without hypocrisy, and allowing Him to guide every step. God told Abraham,

"I am God Almighty; walk before Me and be blameless" (Genesis 17:1).

God gave this command to Abraham, calling him into a covenant of obedience and faith.

Commit yourself to walking before God in obedience, just as Abraham did.

2. To Follow Him

Obedience is also the willingness to follow God wherever He leads, regardless of personal plans or convenience. It requires trust and surrender to His guidance. Jesus said to His disciples,

> *"If anyone desires to come after Me, let him deny himself, and take up his cross daily, and follow Me" (Luke 9:23).*

To follow Christ means to lay down your preferences, ambitions, and sometimes comfort, and go where He leads. The disciples left everything – jobs, family, and security – to follow Jesus. Their obedience positioned them to be used mightily for God's purposes (Matthew 4:19-20).

Commit yourself to following God's plan no matter what happens.

3. To Act on His Command

True obedience requires not just hearing but acting on God's Word. Responding promptly and completely, even when it's inconvenient or costly.

> *"Whatever He says to you, do it" (John 2:5).*

Mary spoke these words at the wedding in Cana, and the servants' obedience led to Jesus' first recorded miracle. Obedience unlocks the supernatural.

Commit yourself to acting promptly on God's instructions.

4. To Learn His Ways

Obedience is not just about following commands; it involves a commitment to understanding God's nature and values. As you learn His ways, obedience becomes your default response.

> *"He made known His ways to Moses, His acts to the children of Israel." (Psalm 103:7).*

Israel saw what God did, but Moses understood why He did it, because he pursued God's heart.

David was described as a man after God's own heart (Acts 13:22). He spent time seeking God's ways, which enabled him to govern with divine wisdom and spiritual insight.

Commit yourself to seek, know, and walk in God's ways.

5. To Submit to Your Assignment

Obedience also means accepting and fulfilling the specific assignment God has given you. Each believer has a divine calling, and obedience is the pathway to fulfilling it.

> *"I have glorified You on the earth. I have finished the work which you have given me to do" (John 17:4).*

Jesus modeled perfect obedience by completing His assignment, even to the point of death. Jonah initially ran from God's assignment to preach to Nineveh. His disobedience led to disaster. But when he finally submitted, an entire city repented (Jonah 3:3-5).

Please find your assignment and give yourself to accomplish it fully. Stop admiring others, develop your talents and gifts, and engage them in serving the Lord. I watched a young man on YouTube play the keyboard so skillfully that it blew my mind. Then I read someone's comment, "O God, can't you give me the talent this young man has?" I responded, "You have your own talent. Develop it, and people will admire you as well."

Are you sitting there admiring others while your talent is buried? Could it be that you have abandoned your divine assignment because you think God did not give you the best one? It is a curse always to covet what others have. Eru (a popular Cameroonian dish) has an irresistible aroma when well-prepared. My wife does it very well, and I enjoy eating it at least once a week. Very few of those who savor Eru can slice it and cook it well. Slicing Eru is done by experts. Like Eru, a raw talent is not particularly attractive. But when it is developed, it becomes an attraction.

Friend, take on your assignment and work diligently to accomplish it. That is obedience. God has given you what is best for you. In the parable of the talents, Jesus said, the master, *"Gave to each according to his ability.* Stop desiring what others have; you will be frustrated. Instead, develop what you have, and you will be happy.

Obedience May Be Costly

Obedience may appear costly, but the result is priceless. When God instructed Abraham to sacrifice Isaac, it was not an easy task. But when he obeyed, he received a transgenerational blessing for his family (Genesis 22). Friend, God is going to ask you to do something challenging to establish the blessing in your family. You must be willing to obey fully and promptly.

Prompt obedience to divine instruction gives you access to the blessing and fresh instructions. God stops instructing those who are not willing to obey His voice. Saul, who had been receiving explicit instructions from God, went into a period of spiritual black out during which he no longer received divine instructions because he had been disobedient (1 Samuel 28:6). Sadly, he committed suicide out of frustration. The only thing that will guarantee your capacity to hear from God is your obedience. If you stop obeying, you will soon lose your spiritual network.

Years ago, while I was trusting God and praying for a car, I received an instruction one Sunday morning to give my one-month salary to a visiting preacher, who was ministering in a program in our church. I had never done such a thing before. Several thoughts began to run through my mind: "How will my family survive during that month?" "What if nothing happens?" I shared with my wife, and we decided to obey the Lord. We gave the money and got the car we had been praying for that same month.

I have learned during my thirty-three-year walk with the Lord that whatever He wants to multiply in our lives, He asks us to surrender it to Him. It is like sowing a grain of corn into the ground. When it dies, it multiplies (John 12:24-25). Abraham gave one to Isaac and received children as numerous as the sand. God gave His one and only Son, and received multitudes of children into His Kingdom.

God will surely ask you to release certain things to Him, just because He wants to bless your family. Be willing to do it immediately. Let nothing be too big for you to give for His work. The demand may be painful, but the reward will be glorious. Do it!

How To Develop A Life of Obedience

Developing a life of obedience requires daily surrender, intentional discipline, and a heart that seeks to honor God above all. Obedience doesn't happen overnight; it's a habit formed over time by walking closely with Jesus Christ. Below are a few steps that can help you:

1. Develop a Listening Heart

Obedience starts by hearing God clearly. You can't obey when you are disconnected from His instructing and guiding voice.

In 1 Samuel 3:1-10, we see the young prophet Samuel learning to know God's voice and to do his will. As a child, Samuel responded,

> **"Speak, Lord, for your servant is listening" (1 Samuel 3:9).**

He cultivated the habit of listening, which made him a faithful prophet.

You must develop the habit of listening to God. When the Holy Spirit led me to start practicing listening, my ministry took on a new dimension. Listening to God has become a habit. It is the first thing I do when I wake up. I have noticed that God's voice is very clear to me between 3 am and 6 am. So, I wake up every night and just listen to Him. It is awesome.

Friend, spend time daily listening to Him and journaling what He tells you.

2. Obey Immediately and Fully

Obey God's instructions promptly and fully, because delayed obedience and partial obedience are classified as disobedience.

When God spoke to Abraham in the night to sacrifice Isaac, the Bible says,

> **"[He] rose early in the morning, saddled his donkey, and took two of his young men with him, and his son Isaac. And he cut the wood for the burnt offering and arose and went to the place of which God had told him" (Genesis 22:3).**

His prompt obedience opened a door of blessing to His family.

Don't wait to feel ready to execute a divine instruction. When God speaks, act promptly. Delayed obedience often leads to missed blessings.

3. Obey in Small Things

Faithfulness in little leads to much. Before fighting Goliath, David obeyed his father by tending sheep and delivering food. God used those small acts of obedience to prepare him for kingship (1 Samuel 17:20, 34-37).

As God's servant, do the menial assignments committed to your hands without complaining. God will use them to prepare you for bigger things. You wouldn't believe your eyes if you saw where I started the ministry in Bafang, West Region of Cameroon. My mother wept when she visited me for the first time in the abandoned house where I was trying to plant the new Church. I looked very pale from fasting and hardship, and the house was terrible. In those days, Bafang people wouldn't rent their homes out to the Church, so we had no choice but to settle in an abandoned, incomplete building. She said she would have taken me away if not for the fact that she was convinced that I was in God's will. My family is enjoying the fruit of that labor today.

Be diligent in your daily responsibilities. See them as assignments from God.

4. Obey Even When It's Difficult or Costly

True obedience is tested in hard choices. In Gethsemane, Jesus obeyed even when it meant dying on the cross (Luke 22:42). His obedience brought salvation to the world.

Dietrich Bonhoeffer, who had escaped the threats of the Nazis in Germany and sought refuge in the U.S.A., was asked by God to return home to strengthen the believers. He obeyed God and was killed by Hitler, but he left a legacy of courage and conviction to the world.

Ask the Holy Spirit for strength to obey even when it's unpopular, painful, or risky.

5. Stay Accountable and Teachable

Obedience grows in community and mentorship. Elisha followed Elijah closely, obeying his instructions until he received a double portion of the anointing (2 Kings 2).

Today, some have missed the mark because they chose to become bosses without learning to serve. A good leader is first and foremost an excellent servant.

Submit to a spiritual mentor or accountability partner. Let others help you stay faithful.

In Summary

Obedience to God's instruction is a vital key to unlocking His blessings. Your obedience creates a ripple effect that impacts not only your children but also future generations. Choosing to follow God, even when it's difficult, is a sacrifice that opens doors for your family's promotion.

Now is the time to fully surrender your heart to God and let the Holy Spirit fill you with the spirit of obedience. Be more committed than ever to spend your life doing God's will, and teaching your family to follow His ways. When you do, God's blessings will never stop flowing into your family.

PRAYER POINTS

Thanksgiving:

1. *Father, thank You for the gift of Your Word that directs our lives and families, in Jesus' name.*

2. *Thank You, Lord, for every blessing we have received through obedience to Your instructions, in Jesus' name.*

3. *We thank You for the example of Jesus Christ, who obeyed even unto death and brought salvation to humanity, in Jesus' name.*

4. *Thank You, Father, for giving us the Holy Spirit, the Spirit of obedience, who enables us to do Your will, in Jesus' name.*

Repentance and Consecration:

5. *Father, forgive us for every act of disobedience and rebellion against Your Word, in Jesus' name.*

6. *Lord, we repent of delayed obedience and partial obedience that has hindered our blessings, in Jesus' name.*

7. *Father, have mercy on us for making our own plans without seeking Your direction, in Jesus' name.*

8. *Lord, remove every hardness of heart and give us a heart of flesh that delights in Your will, in Jesus' name.*

9. *Father, we consecrate ourselves and our families afresh to follow You fully, in Jesus' name.*

Obedience and Divine Direction:

10. *Lord, teach us to obey Your instructions promptly and completely, in Jesus' name.*

11. *Father, give us discernment to recognize Your voice and follow it without fear, in Jesus' name.*

12. *Lord, help us not to compare ourselves with others but to follow Your unique plan for our lives, in Jesus' name.*

13. *Father, give us courage to obey You even when Your instructions seem difficult, in Jesus' name.*

14. *Father, we receive grace to submit to divine timing and wait for Your appointed seasons, in Jesus' name.*

15. *Lord, order our steps as families so we may walk in Your will daily, in Jesus' name.*

16. *Father, may our obedience unlock generational blessings for our children and grandchildren, in Jesus' name.*

Victory Over Disobedience and Rebellion:

17. *Father, deliver us from the spirit of disobedience working in this generation, in Jesus' name.*

18. *By the blood of Jesus, we break every yoke of rebellion in our family line, in Jesus' name.*

19. *Lord, silence every voice that entices us to stray from Your will, in Jesus' name.*

20. *Father, baptize us with the Spirit of obedience to conquer rebellion, in Jesus' name.*

21. *We declare that disobedience will not ruin our family destiny, in Jesus' name.*

Family Commitment and Assignments:

22. *Father, help our families to raise altars of obedience and holiness, in Jesus' name.*

23. *Lord, make our homes places where Your will is honored above all else, in Jesus' name.*

24. *Father, reveal to each family member their divine assignment and help them fulfill it, in Jesus' name.*

25. *Lord, help us to develop the gifts and talents You've given us instead of envying others, in Jesus' name.*

26. *May every member of our family live to glorify You through obedience, in Jesus' name.*

27. *Lord, let our obedience establish strong foundations of blessing for future generations, in Jesus' name.*
28. *Father, use our family's obedience as a testimony to others, in Jesus' name.*

Costly but Rewarding Obedience:

29. *Father, give us strength to obey even when it is painful, in Jesus' name.*
30. *Lord, help us to surrender anything You ask of us, knowing You will multiply it, in Jesus' name.*
31. *Father, may our sacrifices of obedience open doors for generational blessings, in Jesus' name.*
32. *Lord, give us faith like Abraham to trust You even when instructions don't make sense, in Jesus' name.*
33. *Father, empower us to obey You rather than follow the fear of men, in Jesus' name.*
34. *Father, may our obedience be a foundation of blessing that outlives us, in Jesus' name.*

Arrest Satanic Attacks

35. *Father, cut off every hand of death raised against me or members of my family, in Jesus' name.*
36. *I rise against every attack organized to frustrate my destiny, in Jesus' name.*
37. *Father, let Your light expose all secret plans against me, in Jesus' name.*
38. *Evil hands lifted against me shall wither, in Jesus' name.*
39. *Let the eyes of my enemies be opened to see who I am in Christ, in Jesus' name.*
40. *Lord, clothe me with Your mercy and divine favor, in Jesus' name.*
41. *Father, anoint me to flourish where others fail, in Jesus' name.*

Prophetic declarations:

42. *My life shall not be scattered by demonic storms, in Jesus' name.*
43. *We declare that our families shall walk in obedience and enjoy divine elevation, in Jesus' name.*
44. *We prophesy that no spirit of rebellion will overtake our children, in Jesus' name.*
45. *Our homes shall be known for obedience, righteousness, and divine favor, in Jesus' name.*

Cameroon:

46. *Father, thank You for preserving the nation of Cameroon through past challenges and crises, in Jesus' name.*

47. *Forgive the Church where we have been silent, passive, or complicit in evil, in Jesus' name.*

48. *Let the blood of Jesus speak mercy over every legal ground the enemy has against Cameroon, in Jesus' name.*

49. *Lord, we release the blood of Jesus over every region in Cameroon during this election season, in Jesus' name.*

50. *Send Your angels to patrol our borders, cities, and polling stations, in Jesus' name.*

Chapter 4
Days 10-12

Raising Godly Children

"Train up a child in the way he should go; even when he is old, he will not depart from it" (Proverbs 22:6).

Jan Blaustone, author of *The Joy of Parenthood*, says, "The best way to secure your future is to invest time in your children." This corroborates the common saying that "Children are the leaders of tomorrow." This means that if we fail to train our children today, the future is at risk. I know business giants whose empires collapsed after their passing because their children were unprepared to carry on the legacy. The future of any family rests in its children. If you fail to impart what you carry to your children or train them to serve God, then your family has no future. A true family legacy lies in the values we instill in our children.

Dear parent, to neglect the training of your children is to endanger the future of your family, community, Church, and nation. Failing to train your children may deprive them of their God-ordained destiny. A Christian mother once remarked, *"Children who reach adulthood with undisciplined wills and unchecked passions will usually follow paths God condemns."* Today, many are zealously serving the devil because no one guided them in the way of the Lord or instilled in them values for responsible living when they were young.

Every great achiever today was coached and mentored by someone. I am deeply indebted to my parents for the time and investment they poured into my life.

The Best Way to Influence Your Children

The most effective way to influence your children is to live as a true disciple of Christ before their eyes—model the life you want them to embrace. Dr. Mike Murdock says, *"Children observe. They absorb. They are like containers. In their ears we deposit faith or fear, victory or defeat, motivation or depression."*

I learned this powerful lesson from my mother when I was a child: *"Always act on any new spiritual truth you discover right away."* That principle has become a cornerstone of my growth in every area of life over the years. I love reading to discover new ideas that can improve my life. I quickly apply the new things I learn through reading and traveling.

Pastor Nick Vujicic once said, *"Do your best and God will do the rest."* As parents, when we truly give our best, we create a lasting, godly influence in our children's lives for His glory. Research consistently shows that children whose parents actively live out their Christian faith are far more likely to become committed believers themselves.[5] In contrast, studies reveal that children from homes where parents attend church but lack a deep spiritual commitment are significantly less likely to develop a genuine faith in Christ.[6]

I Ate Salad for the First Time

Mummy had just returned from the annual women's retreat of the Full Gospel Mission Cameroon, held that year in Bamenda. She came back beaming with joy and bursting with fresh ideas to transform our family life. The fire in her spirit was contagious. You could see she had truly encountered God.

Without wasting time, she sprang into action. "The retreat taught us that a family that prays together *and eats together* stays strong," she told my father with conviction. "It's time we start eating as a family." Though we already had the habit of praying and reading the Bible together each morning, mealtimes were a different story. Daddy ate alone at the only small table in the house, while we children usually sat on the floor in the kitchen or living room. I still don't know where Mummy used to eat. Probably in the kitchen while multitasking.

To our surprise, Daddy agreed right away. "That makes sense," he said, nodding. "I'll get a proper dining table made for the family." Soon, a carpenter delivered a brand-new wooden table with matching chairs. We were excited, but a greater surprise was yet to come. That evening, Mummy said with a smile, "Today, I'm serving something special; *salad!*" "Salad?" we echoed, confused. We had never heard of it before. Cabbage was not part of the daily menu in our remote village. Don't mention lettuce. It had never been seen in Bechati village. Still, we were curious.

Each of us took a seat at the new table for the first time, watching in anticipation as Mummy served plates filled with something green and colorful. We picked up our spoons with a mix of wonder and hesitation, then took our first bites.

"It's crunchy!"

"Tastes different... but nice!"

"Is this what people in the city eat?"

That meal was unforgettable. From that day on, whenever Mummy could find cabbage and the right ingredients, she surprised us with her special salad. It became a symbol of something more than food. It marked a shift in our home.

Mummy's passion to live out God's Word had brought us into a new rhythm of life. We weren't just eating differently; we were growing stronger as a family, gathered around a table, sharing food, laughter, and love. Something rare in our village, but now a treasure in our home.

The Only Giant Bible in the Village

During one of their trips to Bamenda for a church program, my parents received a powerful teaching on the importance of introducing children to God's Word from infancy, primarily through picture Bibles. Deeply inspired, they didn't hesitate. They invested in what became a treasure in our home: a giant illustrated Bible. I have never seen a children's Bible bigger than that one till today. It was the only one of its kind in our entire community.

At a time when no household had a TV set, this Bible became the main attraction for the children in our neighborhood. Day after day during the holidays, kids from all around would flock to our house, eager to see the vivid illustrations and hear the stories behind them. We'd gather for hours, flipping through the pages, moving from Noah's ark to David and Goliath, from the birth of Jesus to His miracles.

Looking back, I know without a doubt that it was no coincidence that all of us in the family are serving God today. That Bible wasn't just a book; it was a seed. Our parents were intentional about planting the Word of God in our hearts from an early age, and that seed has continued to bear fruit.

Not long ago, someone who had known our family back then and hadn't seen me in over thirty years said, "Godson, it's no surprise you became a pastor. You followed the path your parents laid before you." Indeed, they did more than tell us about God; they showed us the way.

My Parents Wouldn't Let Us Move Anyhow

My parents were so committed to raising us in a godly manner that they wouldn't let us leave home. In those days, my Aunty, who had lived with my parents when I was born and took care of me, wanted me to visit her in Douala, Cameroon, during the summer holiday. She tried in vain, and my parents will not yield. The reason they refused to let me go spend the holiday with her will shock you. They said that since she was not married and was not a believer, I would be exposed to several negative things that could pollute me. I went to spend time with her only after she got married, when I was in form two in secondary school.

Years later, my younger brother Daniel was sent to live with a family in Bamenda to attend secondary school. When the young man returned home after a year away from my family, my parents noticed that the environment had had a negative impact on him. They decided to withdraw him from Bamenda, and he went back to live with them in the village to continue his studies. Today, Daniel is a PhD holder and a notary in the State of Texas, U.S.A., as well as the founder of Restoration Heights Ministries, which has five Churches in Nigeria.

My parents believed that the first thing to do with a child is to establish a strong relationship with God before anything else. It is not a surprise that all their children are serving God passionately.

Mom Was Strict

She was a strict disciplinarian – firm, watchful, and intentional. In a village where many parents allowed their children to roam freely and even served them alcoholic drinks, my mother stood out. She made it clear to everyone: *"Don't you ever give my children any alcohol. Not even a taste." Some of my siblings have never tasted alcohol.*

Mom watched over us like a mother hen guarding her chicks from a circling hawk. We didn't just go anywhere or do anything; we lived by a schedule. She monitored our movements, set boundaries, and made sure we stayed within them. The troublemakers in our community knew they shouldn't loiter around our house. Even though no physical fence existed, the atmosphere around our home was one of discipline and respect.

We were six boys and one girl, plus other children who lived with us. My cousin Dorothy, the only grown-up girl in the house, was especially protected. When any of the boys began to show undue interest in her, Mom addressed it head-on. "Stay away from my daughter or else you will be in trouble with me," she would say bluntly. They didn't dare because they feared her. And Dorothy felt safe.

As we boys grew older, she began addressing another potential threat: the local girls with questionable intentions. "I'm warning you," she told one boldly, "If I ever see you hanging around my son, I will deal with you!" Her presence was commanding, and her words were never ignored.

I recall a defining moment during one of my school holidays when I was in Form Two. I had gone to the football field near our house to play with friends. Usually, she would call out after a while, *"Godson! Come back to the house!"* But this time, no call came. I played for as long as I liked and eventually returned home on my own. Puzzled, I walked into the kitchen where she was cooking.

"Mom," I asked, "Why didn't you call me like you always do? You just let me play until I came home on my own."

She turned and smiled.

"You're in Form Two now," she said gently. "You're growing up. I want to see if you can make the right choices."

In that moment, I realized that all her discipline, all her constant supervision, wasn't just control; it was training. She was raising men, not boys. And that intentional discipline shaped the course of our lives.

Looking back, I thank God for a mother who set boundaries, stood her ground, and taught us to live by godly principles in a world full of compromise.

Role Models in Our Home

At home, we didn't just hear about the Christian life; we saw it lived out daily by our parents. One of the strongest lessons Mom taught us was her profound dislike of lies. She detested dishonesty with a passion and went to great lengths to instill truthfulness in us. If you told the truth, even after misbehaving, she was more likely to forgive you. That principle shaped our hearts from an early age. Dad also reinforced this with his favorite phrase: *"Speak the truth and shame the devil."* He repeated it so often that it became a chant among us children. The kids in the primary schools where he taught nicknamed him, "Speak the truth and shame the devil." Truth-telling wasn't just a rule in our house; it was a way of life.

We had a strong family altar. Every morning before heading out, we gathered to pray and meditate on God's Word. On some days, we even fasted together. During those times, our parents would lay hands and pray over each of us. On weekends, especially Saturdays and Sundays, Dad encouraged us to meet with God personally. That habit continues in my own home to this day.

One of the most impactful things I saw growing up was the way Dad loved and honored his wife. Their marriage has deeply influenced mine. They celebrated their 50th wedding anniversary in December 2020, and I still admire their bond. I learned from Dad how to care for my wife in practical ways. He bought everything for Mom – clothes, shoes, handbags, perfume, jewelry, and even her underwears. Because of that example, I too take joy in shopping for my wife, without shame. Some men shy away from buying personal items for their wives, but I never did, because I saw Dad do it proudly.

Dad and Mom also taught us how to run a home wisely, even on a single income. Dad was a humble primary school teacher. Mom supported the family through a small business. Their strategy was simple yet effective: every end of the month, Dad used his salary to buy foodstuffs in bulk, which Mom then sold. The profits were used to support the family and pay our school fees.

That teamwork was a powerful lesson. Today, my wife and I manage our home and finances together. She serves as our family's accountant and treasurer, and we operate as a team, just like my parents did. And the results speak for themselves.

The Last Words of Mama Maku

Mama Maku was my grandmother. She passed away in 1954. She was one of the more than a hundred wives of the late Fon Lekunze Nembongwe II of the Bamumbu Fondom in Wabane Subdivision, South West Region, Cameroon. By the time she died, she had only one child – my father. He was just fourteen years old when she passed.

Before she died, she left him with these unforgettable words: *"I am leaving you with no brother or sister. Your siblings, your wife, your future – all that you will ever need in life will come from school. So, go to school, and be serious about it."* Those words, my father told us, pierced deep into his heart. He made a personal vow that day to pursue education with all his strength and to provide the best education possible for his children.

That vow became a life mission. Together with my mother, he worked tirelessly, through sweat and sacrifice, to send us to one of the most prestigious schools in the South West Region at the time: Seat of Wisdom College, Fontem. It was no small feat. They labored hard to see three of us through that elite institution. And for that, I deeply honor and salute their unwavering commitment.

Today, my writings bless people across the world. But the seed of that impact was planted in the classrooms during my formative years at Seat of Wisdom College. What you invest in a child's education determines how far that child can go. Inspired by my grandmother's last words and my parents' dedication, I made the same commitment to give my children the very best education possible. And by God's grace, I am doing just that.

Families That Prospered Through Godly Education

Many families have flourished because parents intentionally raised their children in the fear of the Lord and grounded their education in God's Word. Their stories should inspire you to commit to raising your children as carriers of God's blessing and purpose.

1. Abraham's Family

Abraham taught Isaac to trust and obey God (Genesis 22). Isaac passed the blessing to Jacob and Esau (Genesis 27), and Jacob's twelve sons became the twelve tribes of Israel. Because of Abraham's obedience and intentional teaching, God declared:

> *"For I have chosen him, so that he will direct his children and his household after him to keep the way of the LORD..." (Genesis 18:19).*

Abraham's obedience established a generational covenant that continues to have a profound impact on the world today.

Do you realize that every act of obedience, even when it's costly, plants seeds of generational blessing in your family? My father, once mocked by his relatives for following Christ, is now admired by the same family. At a recent family event, one of my uncles said openly, *"Pa Abraham, many of us now admire you and want to have what you have."* It is God's blessing speaking in my family.

2. The Family of Lois, Eunice, and Timothy

Lois (grandmother) and **Eunice (mother)** raised **Timothy** in the faith. They taught him the Scriptures "From infancy." Their genuine faith shaped Timothy to become one of Paul's closest companions and a respected leader in the early church.

> *"I am reminded of your sincere faith, which first lived in your grandmother Lois and in your mother Eunice and... is now in you" (2 Timothy 1:5).*

This is a typical example of **generational discipleship** leading to a fruitful ministry.

Children who are well-trained in the family become potential ministers in God's house.

Today, all of us are ministers in different capacities, impacting this generation because of the sincere faith our parents passed on to us. Prepare your children now to become ambassadors of the Kingdom wherever God will position them tomorrow.

3. The Wesley Family (1669–1742)

Susanna Wesley, known as the "Mother of Methodism," raised 19 children, **including** John and Charles Wesley, whom God used extensively to ignite a revival in England that led to the formation of the Methodist movement, which impacted millions. She educated her children at home, trained them in Scripture, prayer, discipline, and worship. She used a unique method of prayer to connect with God amidst her daily demands. She would pull her apron over her head to create a "Prayer closet," a private space for focused intercession for her children, husband, and the family's needs. This act, known as "Apron prayers," symbolized her commitment to prayer and sent a clear message to her children that she needed uninterrupted time with God. She once said, *"I am content to fill a little space, if God be glorified."* Her private discipline produced public revival through her sons.

My parents must be filled with joy today as they watch me minister with power, seeing firsthand what God is doing through the lives of their children. I'm writing this book to encourage you, dear parent: stay faithful to the godly path. Keep investing in raising your children according to God's pattern. Your labor is not in vain. God will bless them and use them to impact their generation. Don't be tempted to give up or take shortcuts when challenges arise. Stay on the course. Do it God's way, and heaven will back you.

4. Billy Graham's Family

Evangelist **Billy Graham** and his wife, Ruth, both of blessed memory, raised their children with a deep love for the Bible and a commitment to Christian service. Their son, Franklin Graham, now leads Samaritan's Purse and continues evangelistic work globally. Dr. Billy Graham once said, *"A good father is one of the most unsung, unpraised, unnoticed, and yet one of the most valuable assets in our society."* His family legacy has influenced millions of souls across generations.

5. Newton (1643–1727)

He developed the laws of motion and the theory of universal gravitation. Newton was raised in a Christian home and remained a devout believer throughout his life. He studied the Bible extensively and wrote more about theology than he did about science. He believed that scientific discovery was a way to understand God's creation. He said, *"This most beautiful system of the sun, planets, and comets could only proceed from the counsel and dominion of an intelligent and powerful Being."*

6. Michael Faraday (1791–1867)

He laid the foundations of electromagnetism and electrochemistry. Faraday was born into a deeply Christian home and was a member of the Sandemanian Church, a Christian sect that emphasized living by Scripture. His faith shaped his humility, discipline, and dedication to truth. He refused to work on Sundays and considered his scientific work a form of worship. He said, *"The book of nature which we have to read is written by the finger of God."*

Some Families Raised Instruments of Destruction

Throughout history, some of the world's most ruthless dictators and tyrants were shaped not only by politics or ideology but also by the breakdown of their early family environments. Their childhoods were marred by abuse, neglect, violence, or abandonment. These factors deeply influenced their worldview and emotional development. These men, once vulnerable children, eventually became instruments of destruction, bringing unimaginable pain to their nations and generations.

1. Adolf Hitler – *Destroyed by conflict and emotional neglect*

Adolf Hitler, the leader of Nazi Germany and architect of the Holocaust, grew up in a deeply troubled home. His father, Alois Hitler, was a strict, domineering man who often physically abused him. His mother, Klara, though more affectionate, was emotionally overwhelmed and distant. This volatile environment planted seeds of resentment, instability, and hatred in young Adolf. His inability to process rejection and failure, compounded by the lack of emotional nurture, laid the groundwork for his radical ideology and genocidal policies. Hitler's inner wounds became fuel for his destructive ambitions.

2. Joseph Stalin – *Shaped by abuse and survival*
Born as Ioseb Jughashvili, Stalin rose to become the brutal ruler of the Soviet Union, responsible for the deaths of millions through purges, forced famines, and gulags. His early years in Georgia were filled with hardship. His father was a violent alcoholic who frequently beat him and abandoned the family when Stalin was still young. His mother, though religious and determined, raised him in poverty. Stalin developed a hardened heart, a survivalist mindset, and a deep mistrust of others, all traits that became central to his ruthless leadership style.

3. Benito Mussolini – *Rebellion born at home*
Italy's fascist dictator, Benito Mussolini, was raised in a chaotic home. His father, a radical socialist and heavy drinker, was inconsistent in discipline and a poor role model. Anger, rebellion, and academic struggles marked Mussolini's early life. He was expelled from several schools for violent behavior. Instead of being nurtured and guided, his aggressive tendencies were left unchecked. These traits would later manifest in the oppressive and militaristic regime he led, plunging Italy into war and chaos.

4. Saddam Hussein – *Abandonment and anger*
Saddam Hussein, the former president of Iraq, had a childhood steeped in rejection and violence. His father either died or abandoned the family before his birth. His mother, unable to care for him, sent him to live with a brutal and abusive uncle. Growing up in poverty and isolation, Saddam developed deep-seated anger and a craving for control and power. These childhood wounds later translated into a dictatorship marked by fear, executions, war, and repression.

5. Jean-Bédel Bokassa – *Orphaned by violence and grief*
Bokassa, who later crowned himself emperor of the Central African Republic, had a childhood scarred by trauma. In 1927, French colonial authorities, labeling his father a rebel, publicly beat him to death in the

town square of Mbaïki. Just a week later, his mother, devastated by grief, committed suicide. At only six years old, Bokassa was orphaned and left to navigate life alone. This early trauma contributed to his later reign of terror, marked by extreme brutality, corruption, and delusions of grandeur.

We have seen that godly parenting has a profoundly positive transgenerational impact. When children are raised in the fear of the Lord, they not only succeed personally, but they also become vessels of God's blessing to the world.

"The children of your servants will live in your presence; their descendants will be established before you" (Psalm 102:28).

We've also seen that when children grow up in environments of neglect, abuse, or violence, they are often shaped into instruments of destruction, bringing harm to their families and communities.

So, here's the crucial question: "How are you raising the children God has entrusted to your care?" Are you intentionally shaping them to become vessels in God's hands, or are you unknowingly allowing them to become destructive tools in the hands of the enemy? You can choose to make a difference, starting today. Raise them God's way, and leave a legacy of blessing.

Educating Our Children To Become Successful

We must be intentional about educating our children for success. But true success, from God's perspective, goes far beyond academic excellence, wealth, or popularity. It is about walking in God's purpose, bringing Him glory, and impacting others through truth and love. To raise children who are successful by God's standards means nurturing them to live lives rooted in His Word, led by His wisdom, and fully surrendered to His will.

Here are four key principles to achieve that:

1. Teach Them to Fear and Know the Lord

"The fear of the Lord is the beginning of wisdom, and knowledge of the Holy One is understanding" (Proverbs 9:10 NIV).

A godly education begins with instilling the fear of the Lord in our children. In this context, the fear of the Lord refers to the deep reverence and respect for God that leads to obedience. True wisdom starts when children understand who God is and what He expects of them.

Timothy was a young man who became a powerful preacher and a disciple of Paul. His spiritual foundation was laid by his mother, Eunice, and grandmother, Lois (2 Timothy 1:5). They taught him the Scriptures from childhood (2 Timothy 3:15), which anchored his success in ministry.

I read the story of Jonathan Edwards, one of the most brilliant minds in American history. He was a prominent 18th-century American philosopher, theologian, and Congregationalist minister who played a key role in the Great Awakening, a religious revival movement. He was known for his powerful sermons, including "Sinners in the Hands of an Angry God." Jonathan was raised by godly parents who prioritized Bible study, family devotions, and discipline. His descendants included pastors, university presidents, and statesmen, demonstrating that spiritual training yields lasting results.

Billy Graham rightly said, *"The greatest legacy one can pass on to one's children is not money or other material things… but rather a legacy of character and faith."* It is not enough to get your children through the best school; ensure that you have taught them the fear of the Lord.

Throughout the years, I have heard my wife praying continuously for her children with these words, "O God, take over the hearts of my children, and cause them to fear You and walk in my ways." If you sincerely pray for your children and live before them in the fear of God, they will be influenced positively. Do your best and leave the rest to God.

2. Build Their Character Before Their Career

While schools emphasize academic performance and career readiness, Christian parents must prioritize building their children's character. Why? Because character shapes destiny. Talent might secure your child a prestigious job, but only character will help them sustain it.

Take, for example, a recent case in a town in Cameroon, the son of a governor was appointed as a Divisional Officer (D.O.), thanks to his father's influence. However, he was soon removed from the position after becoming a public nuisance, openly smoking marijuana, and even assaulting a village chief. His lack of character cost him the opportunity his background had provided.

Character is the force of your capacity. Focus on developing it. Proverbs 22:6 cautions parents:

"Train up a child in the way he should go, and when he is old, he will not depart from it" (Proverbs 22:6).

"Train" in this scripture is Hebrew *'Chanak,'* which means "To dedicate, inaugurate, initiate, or discipline." This simply means to guide a child's development into godliness, through godly instruction (Deuteronomy 6:6-7), modeling (Proverbs 20:7), and discipline (Hebrews 12:7-11). In other words, provide moral and spiritual direction for your child. To be effective, this must become the way of life in your home.

Integrity, humility, perseverance, respect, and self-control are virtues that enable a child to be successful in the eyes of both God and man. Daniel was a young man of noble character. Even in a foreign land, he refused to defile himself (Daniel 1:8). Due to his integrity and devotion, God gave him knowledge and wisdom surpassing that of his peers, and he served as a high official under different regimes in Babylon.

A 2015 study published in *Child Development* found that children who learn self-control and responsibility early in life have better academic outcomes and healthier relationships in adulthood.[7] The best education without character is a disaster. So, prioritize character development in your children above all.

The early years of a child's life are critical. Parents must be present and intentional about training their children. I chose not to send mine to a dormitory because I wanted to shape their character at home. I am happy with the results I am seeing today. Do everything you can to guide and nurture them before releasing them into the world, just like eagles do. Schools won't build your child's character; that's your responsibility. C.S. Lewis said, *"Education without values, as useful as it is, seems rather to make man a more clever devil."*

3. Prioritize Purpose Over Prestige

Many parents push their children into careers based on money, prestige, or societal approval. But God defines success as fulfilling His purpose – doing what He created us to do. Proverbs 22:6 says,

"Train up a child in the way he should go,"

which in Hebrew means *"According to his path."* This implies that each child has a unique, God-given path. As parents, we're called to discern that path and guide our children accordingly.

Sadly, when parents ignore God's design and force children into paths that look successful on the outside, the results can be tragic. A midwife once shared on Cameroon national radio the story of a frustrated doctor at Yaoundé Central Hospital. One night, she was on duty with him when a complicated labor case required urgent assistance. After repeatedly calling his phone with no response, she went to his office and found him sitting silently, staring into space.

Startled, she asked, "Doctor, why didn't you answer the phone?"

He pointed to the fridge. Inside was the office phone.

Then he quietly said, *"I told my father I never wanted to be a doctor. I hate this job. I'm done."*

He later quit, moved to Britain, and became an accountant, his true passion.

Ephesians 2:10 reminds us that we are God's workmanship, created for specific works He prepared in advance. Every child has a divine assignment. As parents, we must prayerfully guide them to discover their gifts and align their education and training with God's plan, not for self-glory, but for Kingdom impact.

True success doesn't always come from going abroad. Some of the world's wealthiest people are farmers. Cameroon is prophetically positioned to feed nations. While expatriates return to invest in agriculture, many young Cameroonians are chasing dreams overseas.

Don't follow the crowd. Follow God's design.

Every child should be taught a trade. According to the Talmud and Jewish tradition, a father is obligated to teach his child Torah (Scriptures), a trade, and even how to swim. These responsibilities ensure that the child is equipped for both spiritual and practical life. The emphasis on moral development alongside practical skill acquisition produces individuals who are both ethically grounded and functionally competent.[8]

You can do the same for your children. That is what I am doing for mine. Each of them must develop a trade alongside their studies. Some of them are making money while still in school. Also, discover the gifts in your family and build on them. Refine what your parents began. True legacy is created when purpose is preserved and passed on. This is the pathway to family blessings.

4. Model What You Want to Multiply

Children learn more by watching than by listening. Your life is the first Bible your children will ever read. If you want them to live a God-centered, purpose-driven life, model it daily. If you want your family members to follow the Jesus Christ you claim to know, be a practical Christian who lives and loves like Christ.

Paul said,

"Follow my example, as I follow the example of Christ" (1 *Corinthians 11:1).* The Greek word for "Example" is *'mimetes,'* from which we get the English word *mimic.* It means an *imitator or one who follows another's way of life.* In Ephesians 5:1, Paul enjoins the Ephesians, *"Be imitators of God, as beloved children."*

Jesus Himself modeled this principle. In John 5:19, He said,

"The Son can do nothing by Himself; He can only do what He sees His Father doing." Even Christ was shaped by observing the Father. That's divine modeling.

If you want your children and family members to pray, let them see you pray. If you want them to love Scripture, forgive others, or live with integrity, live it first. Don't just teach righteousness; *demonstrate* it. Billy Graham once shared how his parents' consistent prayer and Bible study laid the foundation for his faith. Today, his children and grandchildren continue in ministry, proof of a modeled legacy.

Somebody said, "Children are great imitators. So, give them something great to imitate." What you **live**, not just what you **say**, will multiply in your children. Begin by being the example you want them to follow.

Often, I pray that God will help me be humble and simple like my father. He is a man of peace. I have never seen him quarrel with any man. He serves everybody and prefers to be cheated rather than fight for his rights. His love for Christ is genuine. He reflects the Christian I want to be. I want to be like him. He is my best example.

Do your children desire to love God like you? Your life is a message to them.

A Call to Intentional Parenting

Educating children to be successful according to God is not accidental; it requires prayer, planning, and purpose. It's about raising children who will shine as lights in a dark world, serve as leaders with integrity, and carry God's purposes into every sphere of society.

Don't just aim for your children to succeed in the world. Aim for them to fulfill God's purpose for their lives. That is true success. When I just got married, I often prayed this prayer with my wife, "Father, don't give me a child that would end up in hell." My dream for my family is seeing everybody serving God through our talents and giftings. Like Apostle John,

> **"I have no greater joy than to hear that my children walk in truth" (3 John 1:4).**

PRAYER POINTS
Thanksgiving:

1. *Father, thank You for the gift of children as a heritage and blessing from You, in Jesus' name.*
2. *Thank You, Lord, for the examples of godly parents who inspire us to raise our children in Your ways, in Jesus' name.*
3. *Father, I thank You for the seeds of truth and values already planted in my children, in Jesus' name.*
4. *Lord, I thank You for the promise that if we train up our children in Your ways, they will not depart from them, in Jesus' name.*

Repentance and Surrender:

5. *Father, forgive me for every time I neglected my responsibility to raise my children in godliness, in Jesus' name.*

6. *Lord, have mercy on me for prioritizing worldly success over spiritual foundations for my children, in Jesus' name.*
7. *I repent for exposing my family to ungodly influences knowingly or unknowingly, in Jesus' name.*
8. *Father, I surrender my family afresh to You; let our home reflect Your kingdom, in Jesus' name.*

Raising Children in God's Word:

9. *Lord, help me and my family to delight in Your Word daily, in Jesus' name.*
10. *Father, give my children hunger and thirst for Scripture from an early age, in Jesus' name.*
11. *I declare that my children will walk in truth all the days of their lives, in Jesus' name.*
12. *Lord, raise my children as witnesses of the Gospel wherever they go, in Jesus' name.*
13. *May the seed of God's Word planted in my family bear fruit for generations, in Jesus' name.*

Character and Discipline:

14. *Father, help me to instill godly discipline and values in my children, in Jesus' name.*
15. *Lord, let integrity, humility, and truth become the foundation of my family, in Jesus' name.*
16. *I reject every spirit of rebellion, dishonesty, and disobedience in my children, in Jesus' name.*
17. *Father, help me to balance love and firmness in raising godly children, in Jesus' name.*
18. *I decree that my children will be men and women of character who glorify God, in Jesus' name.*

Purpose and Destiny:

19. *Lord, reveal to me the unique calling and purpose of each of my children, in Jesus' name.*
20. *Father, guide me to nurture the gifts and talents You placed in my children, in Jesus' name.*
21. *My children shall not be forced into wrong paths but shall walk in God's ordained way, in Jesus' name.*

22. *Father, align the education and training of my children with their divine assignment, in Jesus' name.*
23. *Father, help my children to be vessels of honor and fulfill their destinies, in Jesus' name.*

Protection and Preservation:

24. *Lord, shield my children from negative influences, bad company, and ungodly environments, in Jesus' name.*
25. *Father, protect my children from addictions, premature death, and demonic attacks, in Jesus' name.*
26. *Let every evil plan to derail my children's destiny be destroyed, in Jesus' name.*
27. *Father, release Your angels to watch over my children day and night, in Jesus' name.*

Family Unity and Example:

28. *Lord, make my family a model of love, truth, and godliness to others, in Jesus' name.*
29. *May my life be an example that inspires my children to follow Christ, in Jesus' name.*
30. *Father, help my spouse and me to walk in unity as we raise our children, in Jesus' name.*
31. *Lord, heal any broken relationships between parents and children in my family, in Jesus' name.*
32. *May my home always be an atmosphere of prayer, worship, and love, in Jesus' name.*

Impact and Generational Blessings:

33. *Father, let my children rise as lights in their generation, in Jesus' name.*
34. *Father, make my family a channel of blessing to our community and beyond, in Jesus' name.*
35. *Father, let my children grow to raise godly families that continue this legacy, in Jesus' name.*
36. *Father, let the blessing of Abraham manifest in my family, in Jesus' name.*
37. *We receive priestly blessings over our family, in Jesus' name.*
38. *Let every seed our family has sown produce an abundant harvest, in Jesus' name.*
39. *Our tithes and offerings shall speak blessings over our entire household, in Jesus' name.*

Prophetic Declarations:

40. *My children shall influence nations with wisdom, truth, and righteousness, in Jesus' name.*

41. *I decree that my children will surpass me in impact and Kingdom service, in Jesus' name.*

42. *My family will not produce instruments of destruction but carriers of God's glory, in Jesus' name.*

43. *The blessing of Abraham shall flow through my lineage, in Jesus' name.*

44. *I declare that my children shall be taught of the Lord, and great shall be their peace, in Jesus' name.*

45. *I decree that no member of my family shall depart from the faith, in Jesus' name.*

Cameroon:

46. *We declare that no evil shall spread from the North, South, East, or West, in Jesus' name.*

47. *Lord, protect innocent citizens from stray bullets, chaos, or political unrest, in Jesus' name.*

48. *We decree divine security for children, women, and vulnerable groups during this season, in Jesus' name.*

49. *Father, raise leaders who love justice and hate oppression, in Jesus' name.*

50. *Let righteousness exalt our nation again, and let sin be exposed and removed, in Jesus' name.*

Financial Integrity and Hard Work

"The righteous who walks in his integrity, blessed are his children after him!" (Proverbs 20:7).

Integrity and hard work are unshakable foundations for building a truly blessed family. In an era where financial shortcuts, corruption, and materialism are often celebrated, establishing a home or a family rooted in honesty and diligence is both biblical and countercultural. These virtues are not just moral ideals; they are **divine principles that sustain generational blessing**.

A blessed family is not defined merely by wealth, but by **peace, legacy, and divine favor**, fruits that grow from the tree of integrity. The Bible speaks clearly to this truth:

"The righteous who walks in his integrity—blessed are his children after him!" (Proverbs 20:7).

Let's consider this verse in other translations:

- *"The righteous man who walks in integrity and lives life in accord with his [godly] beliefs—how blessed [happy and spiritually secure] are his children after him..." (AMP)*

- *"The righteous live with integrity; happy are their children who come after them." (CEV)*
- *"Children are fortunate if they have a father who is honest and does what is right." (GNT)*
- *"It is a wonderful heritage to have an honest father." (TLB)*
- *"God-loyal people, living honest lives, make it much easier for their children." (MSG)*
- *"The good people who live honest lives will be a blessing to their children." (NCV)*

These translations all convey the same powerful truth: a life of integrity leaves behind a legacy of blessings. It makes life better for your children and for generations to come.

Perhaps you're struggling today because of a foundation of dishonesty or corruption that was passed down to you from your family. But you don't have to remain bound by the past. In this chapter, I'll show you how to lay a new foundation of integrity and hard work, one that will reshape your life and the lives of future generations.

Blaming your background won't change your outcome. Responsibility, not regret, is the key. Through Christ, you can break old patterns and build a better legacy. Choosing integrity may be hard, and diligence may feel unrewarded, but in time, it will pay off and bless your family for years to come.

Mr. "Speak the Truth and Shame the Devil"

My father, Lekunze Abraham Tangumonkem, fondly known as "Pa A.T.," was a dedicated primary school teacher. He began his career with Presbyterian Schools, later taught with the Baptists, served in various government schools as a headmaster, and eventually retired as Chief of Bureau at the Basic Education Inspectorate.

As a devoted, God-fearing Christian, he carried out his duties with integrity, discipline, and excellence. He deeply loved his job and prioritized his pupils' well-being above all else. He was highly committed, rarely missing class or taking time off during the school term.

While many teachers and civil servants often traveled to Yaoundé during school days to follow up on promotions or collect unpaid salaries and bonuses, he refused to do so. Instead, he made it a personal rule to handle such matters only during the holidays. This decision came at a cost – delayed processing of his applications and late payments, which caused financial strain for our family. Still, he believed integrity meant doing what was right, even when others didn't.

Daddy believed that shaping character was just as important as teaching academics. That is why one of his most repeated sayings at school was, *"Speak the truth and shame the devil."* Pupils often heard him declare it sternly, especially when correcting misconduct. During moments of discipline, he would repeat the phrase with each stroke of the cane, reinforcing the value of honesty. Over time, this became his signature, and the pupils began calling him *"Mr. Speak the Truth and Shame the Devil."*

It wasn't just a saying; it was a standard he lived by, both at school and at home. At home, *"Speak the truth and shame the devil"* became almost like a chorus he sang to us all the time. Over time, I realized it wasn't just about discipline; his deepest desire was to raise children of integrity. He lived by those words, modeling honesty in both speech and action. He didn't go out without telling us where he was going.

Watching him consistently walk in truth profoundly shaped my view of life and character. His example taught me that true integrity is not just taught, it's lived.

Grandfather's Legacy

My grandfather, Lekunze Nembongwe II, was a king with over 100 wives and hundreds of children. On my father's first day of primary school, twenty-four children from the palace enrolled in the Infant One Class. At birth, he was named Tangu after his maternal grandfather, but the teacher gave him the name Abraham, which he believes was divinely inspired, as it profoundly shaped his life.

Grandfather is remembered as the most successful ruler in the history of the Bamumbu clan. His legacy wasn't just power; it was character. My father often shared two things about his father that left a lasting impression on him. First, he detested bribery and corruption. He handled palace cases with great fairness and refused to be swayed by gifts or influence. In contrast, his brother, his assistant, who helped govern but ruled with deceit and violence, left behind a struggling lineage. Second,

Grandfather refused to use money collected from fines in the palace court to fund his children's education, calling it "Unclean." My father once returned from school after being sent home for unpaid fees. Grandfather showed him money but said, *"This isn't clean money, I won't use it for your studies."* Instead, he sold a pig to cover the fees. That act of integrity profoundly shaped my father's values. His example sowed a seed of honesty and uprightness that continues to influence our family today.

Lost And Found Money

One lesson my mother taught us as kids profoundly shaped how I view other people's money, especially lost money. She firmly insisted we should never use money we found on the road. We had only two options: return it to the rightful owner or give it to God if the owner couldn't be identified. She repeated this so often that I almost thought it was a Bible verse.

As a child, I remember picking up coins and, not knowing who they belonged to, taking them to church and dropping them in the offering basket. I never once used lost and found money for myself. That teaching became part of my moral compass. I was genuinely shocked one day when a young man saw some banknotes on the road and praised God for the "Provision." That response clashed completely with the values I had been raised with.

Over time, I've realized a powerful truth: **what parents believe and consistently practice will shape their children's values.** Whether good or bad, those lessons become part of the children's worldview.

A Faithful Treasurer

Growing up, I noticed that Daddy always served as either a secretary or treasurer in every church or community group he joined. He carried out his duties with transparency and unwavering integrity. While teaching at Government School Bechati, my father also served as an elder and treasurer in the local Full Gospel Mission Church. With no banks in the village, he had to keep church funds at home. Unfortunately, our house was broken into several times, and the church's money was stolen. Each time, my parents repaid the amount from their own earnings.

One Sunday afternoon, a neighbor's son was seen jumping out of my parents' bedroom window, the same day more money went missing. My father confronted the boy's father, who flatly denied the accusation: "My son is not a thief." Despite knowing my father was a devoted Christian, they tried to pressure him into compromising his faith by suggesting a "Juju man" perform rituals to uncover the truth. Instead, my father quietly repaid the stolen money and left the matter in God's hands.

Though his integrity was tested, he refused to compromise, and God honored him. The young man's life eventually ended in ruin, while my father's legacy stood firm.

The Legacy of Hard Work

Our parents were never lazy. They worked hard, and over time, hard work became a family value that shaped our lives. Today, that foundation still influences everything we do. People often ask me, "Pastor, how do you manage to do so much? Do you have longer days than the rest of us?" The answer is simple: I was trained to work hard from childhood.

After school, Daddy would take us straight to the farm. He always set clear goals before we began. For example, "Today, we will plant 30 suckers of plantain before going home." Rain, mosquitoes, or darkness didn't stop him. While we complained, he would calmly say, "Don't worry, we'll soon finish," and he kept going.

One of our most challenging tasks was building fences to keep goats out of our garden. Eric and I would bear the bamboos, while Daddy tied them to stakes. If he noticed a single mistake, he would undo everything and start over. We grumbled and muttered under our breath, but he'd insist: "Let's do a good job." Sometimes, James stood crying and slapping mosquitoes at night, holding a bush lamp to provide light so we could finish.

That informal training built something deep within us. Years later, when I lost the manuscript of a book after my laptop crashed, I was devastated. But then I remembered those fence-building days. I heard the Holy Spirit whisper, "You can start again, and do it better." I made a vow that day: "Even if my computer crashes a thousand times, I'll write again." That mindset has sustained me through 15 years of writing.

Recently, I visited my brother, Dr. Tangumonkem Eric's farm in Dallas, Texas (DITAWA FARM). A geologist and university lecturer, he's passionate about organic farming and now supplies fresh vegetables across the U.S. That evening, we stayed at the farm past 9 p.m. preparing orders. On the way home, he said, *"Thank you, my brother, for pushing me to hit the mark today."* People wonder how someone with his qualifications can work the soil. But the seed was planted long ago.

If we teach our children that hard work is not a curse, but the key to lasting success, we will lay a strong foundation for a blessed and fruitful family.

Integrity and Hard Work

Let's define "Integrity" and "Hard work" from God's perspective before we continue.

1) "Integrity"

The Old Testament word, "Integrity," is translated from the Hebrew *'Tohm,'* which means, "Completeness, wholeness, innocence, blamelessness, or moral purity." Integrity in Hebrew is more than honesty; it conveys inner consistency and loyalty to God's standards, not just external behavior. Integrity serves as a solid foundation for family blessings.

- *"The godly walk with integrity; blessed are their children who follow them" (Proverbs 20:7 NLT).*

A parent's integrity brings blessings that pass on to their children.

- *"Happy is the person who honors the Lord, who takes pleasure in obeying his commands. The good man's children will be powerful in the land; his descendants will be blessed" (Psalm 112:1-2 GNT)*

Righteous living leads to strong and blessed families.

- *"If you follow me with integrity and godliness… I will establish your dynasty forever" (1 Kings 9:4-5NLT).*

God links a lasting family legacy to personal integrity.

2) "Hard Work"

The Old Testament word, "Work," is translated from the Hebrew *'Ah-mahl,'* which means, "Toil, labor, effort, painful work, or burdensome exertion." It describes not just physical labor but also the emotional and mental effort involved in diligent work.

- *"Work and you will earn a living; if you sit around talking, you will be poor" (Proverbs 14:23 GNT).*
- *"Lazy people are soon poor; hard workers get rich" (Proverbs 10:4 NLT).*

Hard work is God's pathway to prosperity and family provision. Laziness leads to lack. Growing up, I saw that children of lazy parents often suffered. If poverty runs in your family, laziness may be the root. Break it, or live under its grip.

- *"Wealth from get-rich-quick schemes quickly disappears; wealth from hard work grows over time" (Proverbs 13:11 NLT).*
- Lasting wealth comes from steady, honest labor. Cheating people to get rich brings curses on the family.
- *"Whoever refuses to work is not allowed to eat" (2 Thessalonians 3:10 GNT).*

Hard work is not just a virtue—it is a requirement for survival and dignity.

Integrity protects the fruit of your labor. Hard work positions you to receive divine increase. Together, they are the covenant pathways to generational blessing.

Biblical Families Blessed Through Integrity and Hard Work
The Bible has a record of several families that were blessed spiritually through their practice of integrity and hard work.

1. Abraham – *A man of integrity*
In Genesis 14:17-24, Abraham had just defeated four powerful kings and rescued his nephew Lot, returning as a conquering hero with the spoils of war rightfully his. Yet, as a man of integrity, he chose to honor God first by paying a tithe to Melchizedek:

> *"Then Melchizedek king of Salem brought out bread and wine. He was priest of God Most High, and he blessed Abram... Then Abram gave him a tenth of everything." (Genesis 14:18–20, NIV)*

This marks the first recorded tithe in Scripture, not given out of obligation, but out of gratitude. Abraham acknowledged that the victory came from God, not his own strength. Do you show integrity by honoring God with a tithe of your income?

Furthermore, Abraham refused to enrich himself through corrupt alliances or pagan rewards:

"I have raised my hand to the Lord... that I will accept nothing belonging to you, not even a thread or the strap of a sandal..." (Genesis 14:22-23, NIV)

He humbly rejected self-glorification and chose dependence on God for his prosperity. He did not exploit his victory for personal gain but remained morally pure and spiritually focused. In your financial dealings, do you reject dishonest gain because you fear the Lord?

Abraham also treated his nephew Lot with profound integrity (Genesis 13). In a dispute they had, he demonstrated it by choosing peace over personal rights, allowing Lot to pick land first despite being the elder and rightful heir. He refused to exploit Lot's selfish choices and showed moral restraint. When Lot was captured, Abraham risked his life to rescue him without resentment or demands. Even after the rescue, he let Lot return to Sodom, respecting his free will while still interceding for him in prayer with compassion and humility.

How do you treat the vulnerable family members under your care – orphans, widows, step-siblings, and others who depend on you? A woman once came to us for prayer over a painful family matter. Before their father died, he appointed the youngest brother as the family administrator and left him the house in the village. However, their eldest brother, who earns millions of Francs CFA monthly, rejected the will, acquired a traditional title, and forcibly evicted his jobless younger brother from the house. Greed can drive people to great wickedness, even against their own blood.

Do you desire your family to be blessed like Abraham's? Then treat every member with honor, fairness, and integrity, especially those who are vulnerable. God sees, and He rewards justice.

2.   Isaac – *An industrious man*

Isaac's family was blessed not just because of the Abrahamic covenant but through hard work and persistence. During a severe famine, he didn't wait for ideal conditions; he planted crops and reaped a hundredfold because **God blessed his labor** (Genesis 26:12-13). He became very wealthy, attracting the envy of the Philistines. But note that his blessing followed action.

He also demonstrated persistence by re-digging the wells his father had dug (Genesis 26:15ff). When local herders opposed him, he didn't fight back; instead, he kept digging until he found peace and room at Rehoboth (Genesis 26:22).

Isaac's household also reflected a culture of work. Esau was a skilled hunter, and Jacob managed livestock. This shows that Isaac passed on a strong work ethic to the next generation. His life teaches that God blesses faith-filled, diligent labor, especially in hard seasons.

Do you want lasting family blessings? Follow Isaac's example: sow in faith, work hard, persist in opposition, and trust God to multiply your efforts.

3.   The Rechabites – *A model of faithfulness*

The Rechabites are a powerful example of how **generational integrity** leads to **divine favor and lasting blessing**. Descendants of Jonadab, son of Rechab (2 Kings 10:15-23), appear in Jeremiah 35 as an example of faithfulness. For generations, they obeyed their forefather's command not to drink wine or settle permanently, practicing loyalty and discipline. Even when Jeremiah tested them with wine in the temple, they refused, showing moral courage and unwavering integrity under pressure.

Their obedience wasn't based on convenience but on conviction. In response, God honored them:

> ***"Jonadab son of Rechab will never fail to have a descendant to serve me" (Jeremiah 35:18-19).***

While many families in Israel faced judgment for disobedience, the Rechabites were rewarded with a perpetual legacy of service and favor. Their story teaches us that steadfast integrity, especially when passed from one generation to another, brings lasting recognition and favor from God.

Your integrity will place God's stamp of favor on your lineage.

4. Ibukun Awosika – *A woman of integrity*

She is a committed Christian, entrepreneur, author, and the first female Chairperson of *First Bank Nigeria*. Known for her unwavering integrity, she built The Chair Centre Group into a respected brand and rose to national prominence through hard work and godly values. She has consistently refused bribes, rejected unethical deals, and boldly lived out her faith in the business world.

At home, she and her husband lead a faith-driven family built on discipline and humility. Her children reflect the same strong values. Ibukun also mentors young entrepreneurs, encouraging them to succeed without compromising righteousness. Through her talks and books like *The Girl Entrepreneurs*, she teaches that integrity, not manipulation, is the true door to lasting success. Her life is a model of how Christian principles and professional excellence can thrive together in the marketplace.

5. The Green Family – *Business with integrity*

David and Barbara Green (USA) run Hobby Lobby, a multi-billion-dollar retail chain with over 900 stores. David launched it in 1972 with just $600 and a strong work ethic, crafting picture frames in his garage. From the beginning, he built the company on Christian values and uncompromising integrity. The family honors God by closing all stores on Sundays, sacrificing millions in profit to prioritize rest and worship. Known for radical generosity, they donate up to 50% of profits to ministries, Bible distribution, and education. In 2014, they won the landmark Hobby Lobby v. Burwell case at the U.S. Supreme Court, defending religious freedom. Their influence extends beyond business. The Greens also founded the Museum of the Bible in Washington, D.C., to preserve and promote biblical truth for future generations. Their story shows how faith and integrity can lead to both spiritual and business success.

You can do clean business and prosper abundantly (Job 1:1-3).

Examples of Families Ruined by Dishonesty and Corruption

Here are four notable examples of biblical and modern families that were ruined by dishonesty, corruption, and lack of integrity.

1. **Eli's Family** – *Corrupt spiritual leadership (1 Samuel 2:12-36)*

Eli's sons, Hophni and Phinehas, served as priests in the tabernacle, but they were wicked and corrupt. They disrespected God's offerings, exploited women sexually, and treated sacred duties with contempt. Although Eli was aware of their sinful behavior, he failed to take firm action or remove them from office. His inaction enabled their corruption and dishonored the priestly office entrusted to his family. God responded with a severe judgment: He declared that Eli's lineage would be cut off and that his sons would die on the same day as a sign of His displeasure.

> *"I will carry out against Eli everything I spoke concerning his family, from beginning to end" (1 Samuel 3:12).*

This tragic story reveals that dishonesty and corruption in leadership, especially within the family, invite divine judgment on a family. Eli's failure to discipline his sons led to the downfall of his household and the loss of generational spiritual influence.

Some families are cursed because their parents desecrated holy things. Your family cannot prosper when you steal God's money and corrupt the priesthood.

2. **Ananias and Sapphira** – *Financial Dishonesty (Acts 5:1-11)*

Ananias and Sapphira were a married couple in the early church who agreed to deceive the apostles and the Holy Spirit. They sold a piece of land and pretended to donate the full proceeds to the church, while secretly keeping part of the money.

Their sin wasn't in keeping a portion, but in lying to appear more generous and spiritual than they truly were. The Holy Spirit exposed their hypocrisy through Peter.

> *"You have not lied just to human beings but to God" (Acts 5:4b, NIV)*

Ananias fell dead immediately, and hours later, Sapphira met the same fate after repeating the lie.

This event sent shockwaves through the early church and stands as a sobering warning about the seriousness of dishonesty, especially when done in agreement within a family. It reminds us that God values truth over appearances and that lying to God brings serious consequences.

3. The Madoff Family – *Financial fraud*

The Madoff family was tragically ruined by the deceitful actions of its patriarch, Bernie Madoff, who orchestrated the largest Ponzi scheme in history, defrauding investors of over $60 billion.

For years, the family enjoyed wealth and status, but the foundation was built on lies. When the fraud was exposed, the consequences were devastating. One son, Mark Madoff, committed suicide, unable to bear the shame. Another, Andrew Madoff, died of cancer under intense public scrutiny. Bernie was sentenced to 150 years in prison, where he later died. The Madoff name became synonymous with fraud, greed, and betrayal.

This tragic story serves as a modern warning that dishonesty, no matter how well-disguised, ultimately destroys families and tarnishes legacies. True success must be built on truth, integrity, and accountability, not manipulation and greed.

These stories clearly demonstrate that while dishonesty may yield temporary gains, it ultimately leads to loss, shame, and destruction, often spanning generations. The Bible is clear,

"He who profits unlawfully brings suffering to his own house, but he who hates bribes [and does not receive nor pay them] will live" (Proverbs 15:27 AMP).

Are you interested in raising a blessed family? You must commit yourself to developing a culture of integrity in your family.

How to Cultivate Integrity and Hard Work in Your Family

Integrity and hard work are essential virtues that shape a family's character, success, and legacy. Talent may open doors, but only honesty and diligence keep them open across generations. These values don't come by chance; they must be intentionally built at home. Here are four practical ways to do that:

1. Lead by Example – *Model what you want to see*

Children learn more from what we do than what we say. If you want to raise a family of honest and hardworking individuals, start by consistently living those values. Jesus said,

"I have given you an example that you should do as I have done to you" (John 13:15). Let your children see you return extra change, admit mistakes, speak the truth, and finish tasks faithfully. Wake up early, show up on time, and keep your word – your daily actions set the standard for the family.

A father who worked as a carpenter once refused a bribe to use lower-quality materials on a building project. Despite financial pressure, he chose to honor God and maintain his standards. Years later, his son, now a successful architect, said, *"I learned to reject corruption by watching my father stand for integrity, even when we had very little."*

To reinforce these values, write a family motto centered on integrity and hard work. Frame it and hang it on your wall. Repeat it often, and let it guide your family culture.

2. Assign Responsibilities and Hold Everyone Accountable

Integrity and hard work grow when family members are trusted with responsibilities and held accountable for the outcomes. Start by assigning age-appropriate tasks, such as teaching young children to make their beds, clean their rooms, help with meals, or manage small budgets. As they mature, give them more responsibility, such as organizing a family event or saving toward a shared goal. This builds discipline, ownership, and a sense of contribution.

Again, Proverbs 22:6 says,

"Train up a child in the way he should go, and when he is old, he will not depart from it."

In my home, we practice what I learned from my parents, we intentionally assign tasks to our children as they grow. Over time, this routine has produced disciplined and responsible individuals who are maturing into adults capable of managing homes, careers, and ministries with excellence. Years ago, I also began teaching them to handle money with integrity. We introduced a family savings scheme called *"Njangi,"* where each child contributes and learns to save. They've also learned that any income they receive, they should honor God with a tithe or first fruit to God, and save a portion. This practice has shaped their attitude toward stewardship, giving, and financial responsibility.

Pew Research data reveals that families who practice budgeting and teach children financial responsibility have significantly higher levels of financial stability and long-term wealth retention.

The principle is simple: Choose the habits you want to see in your family and train them deliberately. Children don't stumble into success; it is built through consistent guidance and example. Integrity and hard work must be sown early to reap a lasting harvest.

3. Celebrate Honesty and effort, Not Just Excellence

Many families unintentionally reward charisma, intelligence, or performance while overlooking honesty and effort. This breeds a culture where appearance matters more than character. But true success is built on integrity, diligence, and perseverance, even when the results aren't perfect.

Be intentional by celebrating the process, not just the outcome: "I saw how hard you worked. I'm proud of your effort." Share examples of people like Ruth, Joseph, Nehemiah, or Nelson Mandela, who rose through integrity.

In Uganda, a boy failed his exam because he refused to cheat. To his surprise, when he got home, his father said, "I'm proud of you. You did what's right." The boy later graduated top of his class, proving that character lasts longer than shortcuts.

When I present school awards, I honor the most improved and most disciplined, not just the best student. I once topped my class, not from effort, but because God gifted me. That was grace, not achievement.

"Better is the poor who walks in integrity…" (Proverbs 19:1). God values integrity above success. Let this be your mindset.

4. Teach Financial Honesty and the Value of Work

Integrity and diligence must be visible not only in our words but in how we manage money and labor within the family. Children need to see financial principles lived out daily. Involve them in basic budget discussions by showing how income is earned, how expenses are prioritized, and how savings and giving are planned. Let them understand that money is not magic; it is the fruit of honest labor and wise choices.

Avoid modeling shortcuts like tax evasion, dishonest dealings, or manipulating systems for gain. Children internalize what they observe. Remember this!

"Wealth gained hastily will dwindle, but whoever gathers little by little will increase it" (Proverbs 13:11 ESV).

What do you want your family to become when you buy certificates for your children and bribe their way into positions they don't merit? I always think that if I swindled money, my children would suffer the consequences.

John Maxwell once shared how he taught his daughter financial responsibility. She started selling candies to her friends, then to the community. He made her keep records of what she bought, sold, earned, and saved. It wasn't about the candy; it was about instilling discipline, stewardship, and dignity in work.

I remember the first time my daughter sold the snacks she had prepared. She was so excited about her earnings. I told her the money she labors for is sweeter than the one Daddy gives. You can assign to each child a small income-generating project, like selling crafts or managing a family petit-business. Let them handle the money, tithe from it, and save part of it. Through this, help them cultivate the values of work, integrity, and responsibility.

Choose Integrity

We have seen that integrity is a sure foundation for a blessed life. It is also the key to breaking evil foundations and reversing generational curses. You cannot continue in the wicked patterns of your ancestors and expect different results. Jesus paid the full price on the cross to make you new.

I challenge you today: embrace the new life in Christ – a life marked by integrity. Yes, corrupt and dishonest people may mock your stand. They may laugh at your refusal to cut corners or take shortcuts. Don't be discouraged. Keep doing what is right. Your reward will come. God is faithful. He blesses honest labor. Your family will be blessed because of your commitment to truth and righteousness.

Financial integrity ensures that blessings endure. A family that works hard, gives generously, and stewards resources wisely reflects the economy of God's kingdom.

As Rick Warren puts it: "Work becomes worship when you dedicate it to God and perform it with integrity."

Let your life be a testimony. Let your integrity become a channel for the revelation of God's glory in your family and beyond.

PRAYER POINTS
Thanksgiving:
1. *Father, thank You for the heritage of integrity and hard work in our family, in Jesus' name.*
2. *Thank You, Lord, for the blessing of honest labor that sustains our household, in Jesus' name.*
3. *Father, I thank You for the legacy of godly values passed down by faithful parents, in Jesus' name.*
4. *Thank You for the promise that the righteous who walk in integrity leave blessings for their children, in Jesus' name.*

Repentance and Mercy
5. *Lord, forgive us for every compromise, dishonesty, or corruption that has brought reproach upon our family, in Jesus' name.*
6. *Father, have mercy on us for every financial shortcut or dishonest gain that has opened doors to curses, in Jesus' name.*
7. *We repent for neglecting diligence and choosing laziness over hard work, in Jesus' name.*
8. *Father, cleanse our family from every wrong foundation of greed, deceit, and manipulation, in Jesus' name.*

Integrity as a Foundation:
9. *Lord, establish my family on the foundation of truth and honesty, in Jesus' name.*
10. *May our children grow up to value integrity above riches, in Jesus' name.*
11. *Father, give us the courage to reject corruption even when it costs us, in Jesus' name.*
12. *Let integrity become the language and culture of our family, in Jesus' name.*
13. *Lord, help us to "Speak the truth and shame the devil" in every circumstance, in Jesus' name.*
14. *May our integrity leave behind a generational blessing, in Jesus' name.*

Hard Work and Diligence:

15. *Father, plant in us the discipline to work hard and reject laziness, in Jesus' name.*
16. *Lord, bless the work of our hands and multiply our efforts, in Jesus' name.*
17. *May our family never be victims of poverty due to slothfulness, in Jesus' name.*
18. *Father, give us persistence to keep sowing and working even in hard seasons, in Jesus' name.*
19. *May our children inherit a strong work ethic and dignity in labor, in Jesus' name.*
20. *Lord, deliver us from the curse of idleness and unfruitfulness, in Jesus' name.*

Break the Foundation of Poverty:

21. *Father, in the name of Jesus, I uproot every evil foundation of poverty laid in my family line, in Jesus' name.*
22. *By the blood of Jesus, I break every generational covenant that ties my family to lack and insufficiency, in Jesus' name.*
23. *Foundational curse of financial struggle and limitation, be destroyed now, in Jesus' name.*
24. *Father, disconnect my household from ancestral patterns of failure, stagnation, and poverty, in Jesus' name.*
25. *Lord, let the fire of the Holy Ghost consume every demonic altar reinforcing poverty in my lineage, in Jesus' name.*
26. *Every spirit of hardship inherited from my father's or mother's house, release my family now, in Jesus' name.*
27. *Father, establish a new foundation of abundance, prosperity, and fruitfulness for my household, in Jesus' name.*
28. *By the power of the cross, I silence every voice from the past crying poverty into our future, in Jesus' name.*
29. *Lord, build for us a foundation of financial integrity, wisdom, and generational wealth, in Jesus' name.*
30. *I declare that poverty is no longer our inheritance; prosperity and divine provision shall be our foundation, in Jesus' name.*

Breaking Foundations of Corruption:

31. *Every evil foundation of dishonesty in my family line, be destroyed, in Jesus' name.*
32. *I break every curse of corruption inherited from my ancestors, in Jesus' name.*

33. *Lord, deliver us from the spirit of greed that ruined families like Ananias and Sapphira, in Jesus' name.*
34. *Every demonic altar sustaining financial dishonesty in my lineage, catch fire, in Jesus' name.*
35. *Father, expose and uproot every hidden practice of deception in our household, in Jesus' name.*
36. *I decree that our family will not end in shame like Eli's household, in Jesus' name.*

Family Training and Example:

37. *Lord, help us to lead our children by example in integrity and hard work, in Jesus' name.*
38. *Father, give us wisdom to train our children in financial honesty and responsibility, in Jesus' name.*
39. *May we celebrate honesty and effort more than shortcuts and false success, in Jesus' name.*
40. *Father, let our home become a school of diligence, stewardship, and excellence, in Jesus' name.*
41. *May our children be known for truth, hard work, and godly success, in Jesus' name.*

Prophetic Declarations:

42. *We declare that our family shall prosper through integrity and hard work, in Jesus' name.*
43. *Our lineage shall never lack men and women of truth and diligence, in Jesus' name.*
44. *We prophesy that dishonest gain will never enter our household, in Jesus' name.*
45. *Our children will surpass us in righteousness, wisdom, and productivity, in Jesus' name.*
46. *Our wealth shall be clean, blessed, and preserved for generations, in Jesus' name.*

Cameroon:

47. *Remove every unrepentant power that exalts itself above Your will, in Jesus' name.*
48. *Raise voices of truth in politics, media, and government that cannot be silenced, in Jesus' name.*
49. *Father, awaken the Church in Cameroon to rise as a prophetic voice at this hour, in Jesus' name.*

50. *Let the altars of prayer and intercession burn day and night across the nation, in Jesus' name.*

Chapter 6
Days 16-18

Break Evil Foundations

"Christ redeemed us from the curse of the law by becoming a curse for us – for it is written, "Cursed is everyone who is hanged on a tree" – so that in Christ Jesus the blessing of Abraham might come to the Gentiles, so that we might receive the promised Spirit through faith" (Galatians 3:13-14).

Can a family be under a curse? Yes, some families are laboring under curses and are being tormented by evil spirits. Such a family needs to break the powers of those satanic powers to enjoy divine blessings.

A curse, in essence, is when God allows Satan to afflict a family due to their sin. In Luke 10:19, Jesus gave us authority to trample on serpents, scorpions, and all the power of the enemy. But when a family turns away from God, they come under demonic oppression. Instead of walking in authority over the enemy, they become victims of torment from evil powers.

Satan uses various demonic forces to torment families that have opened spiritual doors to him through sin. People often report seeing serpents, lions, dragons, or other evil beings attacking them, especially in dreams. These are real spiritual attacks, and many families suffer constant harassment from these forces. If this is your situation, it needs to be addressed.

But take note of this biblical truth:

"*Like a fluttering sparrow or a darting swallow, an undeserved curse does not come to rest" (Proverbs 26:2).*

In other words, no curse comes without a cause. If a family is cursed or facing spiritual oppression, there is always a reason behind it. Satan cannot afflict a family unless he has legal grounds to do so. Take note of this when dealing with family deliverance.

In **Luke 4:6**, Satan told Jesus to bow before him and he would give Him the kingdoms of the world, saying, ***"They have been given to me."*** Who gave them to him? Adam and Eve did. When they sinned, they handed authority over to Satan. Sin opens the door for Satan and his demons to invade a family. When families walk in rebellion against God, they invite spiritual attacks. But thank God, there is a way out through Jesus Christ and His deliverance power.

Let me show you how to break evil foundations in your family and usher in God's blessings. As you read, focus on two things: (1) The cause of your problem. (2) The solution proposed to deal with. After you have identified these two, set aside time to address the underlying issues thoroughly. Mobilize family members who can pray to join you in warfare prayers. Pray like a wounded lion, trusting God to answer your prayer. He will surely answer you.

Welcome to a new beginning in your family.

What Is Wrong With Us?

Family deliverance and restoration often begins with a sincere question: "What is wrong with us?" It's a question only God can help you answer. However, as long as you're comfortable managing your current situation, don't expect much change. I met a man in Yaounde who lived in a single room with his wife and seven children. If you can keep coping like that, God may allow it to continue. But when you can't endure it anymore and cry out to Him, a divine breakthrough is inevitable. As Isaac told his son, Esau:

"You'll live by your sword, hand-to-mouth, and you'll serve your brother. But when you can't take it anymore, you'll break free" (Genesis 27:40 MSG).

It is only those who can no longer take it that can break free. It's the desperate who ask God, "What is wrong with me?" And in Jesus' name, such people break free. Desperation breaks oppression.

I Asked God

In October 1994, I listened to a message preached during the "Fire Conference," in Limbe, Cameroon, organized by Dr. Billy Lubanza that year. I discovered through it that something was seriously wrong with my family. I was a Bible student at the time, unable to pay my school fees. I owned only one pair of shoes and two shirts. Compared to my classmates, my condition was deplorable. I was the only student sent out of class for unpaid fees, and I didn't even have the taxi fare to leave the Bible School campus, at Mile 3 Nkwen, Bamenda - Cameroon.

My younger brother had passed A-levels with flying colors but couldn't move on to the university because of the lack of funds. We were barely surviving. My father, though a trained teacher, earned a bachelor's salary despite being married with children. He had followed up job files in Yaounde for years—nothing ever worked out. Education beyond high school seemed like an impossible dream for our family.

That message pushed me to seek God. I started praying, asking: "Lord, what is wrong with us? Why this poverty and stagnation?" As I pressed on in prayer and study, the Holy Spirit began to reveal foundational issues – curses and bondages in my family that needed to be broken.

After collecting all available data, I gathered my family to seek God in fasting on January 2, 1995. Everyone joined, even Joseph, the youngest, who was just four years old. From 7 a.m. to 7 p.m., we prayed, sang, repented, and cried to God. Something indescribable happened. Ancient gates were lifted. The King of Glory entered our family.

Thirty years later, the transformation is as clear as day and night. God has done wonders in my family. If you know my family, you will bear witness that we are blessed and blessing multitudes.

Family Name Changed

Ten years ago, a lady in her thirties came to my office after reading *Power Must Change Hands, Vol. 1: Dealing with Evil Foundations*, and requested family deliverance. I gave her a program to follow with her family. During the concluding prayer session in their family house, the Holy Spirit prompted me to ask about the meaning of their family name. They told me it meant *"House of Fermentation."* In other words, *"House of Desolation."* I asked why, and they explained that their great-grandparents both had leprosy. Before dying in shame, they named their child (the grandfather of the current family) *"House of Fermentation."* The grandfather was deceased, but his wife was present during the prayer. She told me she had given birth to eleven children, and only three were still alive.

The name painted a vivid picture of the family's condition. It was indeed fermenting. Most members were unmarried, many had children out of wedlock, others died young, and poverty was rampant. The leprosy in their history was a sign of a generational curse.

We ministered to them, and I changed the family name from *"House of Desolation"* to *"House of God,"* just as God has renamed people in Scripture:

> ***"You shall no longer be termed Forsaken, nor shall your land any more be termed Desolate; but you shall be called Hephzibah, and your land Beulah…" (Isaiah 62:4).***

Within two weeks, marriage proposals began to flood in. The lady who brought me to the family told me two responsible men came at the same time, asking for her hand. She settled down with one of them.

Biblical Examples of Families Under Bondage

The Bible shows how the sins of individuals often brought lasting consequences to their families:

1) **The family of Adam:** Adam sinned by disobeying God's command and eating the forbidden fruit (Genesis 3:6-7). Consequently, the entire human race was affected by sin, and death entered the world (Romans 5:12-19).

2) **The Family of Noah:** Ham's disrespectful and sinful behavior towards his father, Noah, led to a curse on him and his seed (Genesis 9:20-27). Noah cursed Canaan, Ham's son, and his descendants were affected (Genesis 9:25).

3) **The family of Abraham:** Abraham's lies about his wife Sarah, saying she was his sister, laid an evil foundation in his family (Genesis 12:10-20, 20:1-18). Abraham's descendants, including Isaac and Jacob, faced similar challenges and responded similarly to their father, Abraham (Genesis 26:1-33, 27:1-46).

4) **The family of Jacob:** Jacob deceived his father, Isaac, to grab his brother Esau's blessing (Genesis 27:1-46). Jacob's descendants, including his sons, faced the consequences of their own sins, including the brothers' jealousy and hatred towards Joseph. They sold Joseph because they hated the idea of him becoming influential, as revealed by the dreams (Genesis 37:1-36).

5) **The Family of David:** David committed adultery with Bathsheba and killed her husband, his military officer, to cover up the sin (2 Samuel 11:1-27). David's sin brought a curse and calamities on his family: the death of his adulterous son with Bathsheba, incest, rape, his son killed his brother, Absalom's rebellion, and the division of the kingdom (2 Samuel 12:1-23, 15:1-37, 18:1-33).

6) **The Family of Ahab:** Ahab polluted the land with idolatry and murdered Naboth to claim his land (1 Kings 21:1-29). His family faced a curse, and his descendants, including his son Joram, were killed brutally (1 Kings 21:20-24, 2 Kings 3:1-27, 9:1-37).

These examples illustrate the biblical principle that the sins of ancestors can have consequences for their descendants. However, it's essential to remember that God is a God of mercy and forgiveness, and He desires to break curses and restore families through repentance and faith.

Contemporary examples of families suffering under curses:

Studies revealed that the following families were laboring under curses.

1) **The Kennedy Family U.S.A.:** The Kennedy family has been plagued by a series of tragic events, including the assassinations of John F. Kennedy and Robert F. Kennedy, as well as the death of John F. Kennedy Jr. in a plane crash. Some attribute this to a curse placed on the family by a woman whom Joseph P. Kennedy Sr wronged.

2) **The Vanderbilt Family U.S.A.:** The Vanderbilt family was once one of the wealthiest families in America, but tragedies, including family feuds, scandals, and untimely deaths, have plagued them. Some attribute this to a curse placed on the family by a rival businessman.

3) **The Habsburg Family:** The Habsburg family, which ruled Austria and Hungary for over 600 years, was plagued by a series of tragic events, including the assassination of Archduke Franz Ferdinand, which led to World War I. Some attribute this to a curse placed on the family by a woman whom Emperor Maximilian I wronged.

4) **The Family of King Sobhuza II of Swaziland:** The curse was said to have caused a series of tragic events, including the death of several of the king's children and grandchildren.

5) **The Family of President Mobutu Sese Seko of Zaire:** President Mobutu, who ruled Zaire (now the Democratic Republic of Congo) from 1965 to 1997, was said to have been cursed by a rival politician whom the president wronged. The curse was said to have caused a series of tragic events, including the death of several of the president's children and the downfall of his regime.

Symptoms of Family Bondage

Here are some probable signs of family bondages. Here, I am pointing out symptoms, not causes. Symptoms will guide you to the causes. For instance, a headache is not a disease but a symptom associated with several diseases, including malaria. Paracetamol is a painkiller that can calm down headaches, but it cannot treat malaria. So, if you focus on eliminating the headache without addressing the underlying malaria, you have not solved the problem.

Poverty is a symptom; laziness, unfaithfulness, or demonic oppression are the causes. The cycle of divorce and remarriage in a family is a symptom; immorality or violence is the cause. Deeper beneath the immorality or violence lies a sin committed that became the legal basis for the curse to stand (Proverbs 26:2). We will see later that the starting point for dealing with family bondages, calamities, or captivities is addressing the sin that laid the evil foundation.

If you think declaring war against the powers of darkness or doing some rituals with salt, water, oil, and a broom is enough to set your family free from a curse, you are just kidding. You must close the door of sin.

Families in bondage needing deliverance have the following symptoms:

1) Family members suffer constantly from mental and emotional breakdowns.
2) Family members repeatedly experience chronic sicknesses, which are hereditary and challenging to treat.
3) Tragic events – assassinations, premature death, accidents, etc., in the family, as mentioned in the families above.
4) Family breakdown. Inability to keep a marriage. Cycles of marriage and divorce. Marital unfaithfulness is rampant among them.
5) Several family members are irresponsible (Indebtedness, drug addiction, drunkenness, gambling, etc.).
6) Prolonged barrenness with different family members. I know a family that has no children. If nothing is done, the family will become extinct.
7) Family misunderstandings and quarrels are common.

8) Family members often struggle to find partners. I know of a family with very beautiful, well-educated ladies in their thirties and forties. None is married. During my twenty-nine years of pastoral counseling, I noticed patterns among people from different tribes in Cameroon. I will not mention names. Often, when people come to me and complain, I ask, "Are you from…tribe?" and they answer yes. It is not a revelation. I have observed the patterns. The patterns I noticed include celibacy among women, irresponsibility among men, immorality, greed, and others.

9) Family members work hard but live in poverty, hand to mouth. I once prayed with a woman who had ten children. None except one who was born again had gone beyond primary school education. They were all servants on the farms, existing from hand to mouth. The father of this lady told her not to marry, so she had those children with different men.

10) Family members are accident-prone.

11) Family members often start good things but rarely finish them (E.g., School dropout, always starting something new).

12) Limitations in life (financially, spiritually, professionally), etc.

13) Family incidents of untimely death, suicides, etc. (Deuteronomy 28).

Sins that open the door to Satan:

If you believe that your family is in bondage, use these points to identify the cause:

1) Disobedience to God's commands: Deuteronomy 28:15-68 says,

> *"However, if you do not obey the Lord your God and do not carefully follow all his commands and decrees I am giving you today, all these curses will come on you and overtake you."*

King Saul disobeyed God's command to destroy the Amalekites. He also turned to idolatry (1 Samuel 15:1-35). As a result, his family was cursed, and his sons were killed in battle.

2. Idolatry and false worship: Exodus 20:3-5 says,

> *"You shall have no other gods before me. You shall not make for yourself an idol in the form of anything in heaven above or on the earth beneath or in the waters below... You shall not bow down to them or worship them; for I, the* LORD *your God, am a jealous God, punishing the children for the sin of the parents to the third and fourth generation of those who hate me."*

The family of Jeroboam, who introduced idolatry in Israel (1 Kings 12:25-33). As a result, his family was cursed, and his son Abijah died.

Today, several families are languishing because of the foundation of idolatry their ancestors laid, and opened the door to demons. Not long ago, a woman came to our office for deliverance prayer. She told us that her father had an altar in their house and often went there to worship at midnight. He would open the window, invoke, and invite demons to his house. Today, the family is miserable. The children of the man are living in abject poverty. When we told her to call her brother in Nkongsamba, she said the man did not own a phone because he lacked the money to get one.

3) Injustice and oppression: Isaiah 10:1-4 says,

> *"Woe to those who decree iniquitous decrees, and to those who dictate unrighteous dictums, to turn aside the needy from justice and to rob the poor of my people of their right, that widows may be their spoil, and that they may make the fatherless their prey!"*

King Ahab oppressed and murdered Naboth to take his vineyard. God cursed his family, and they died from the sword (1 Kings 21:1-29).

My uncle told me about some men in my village several years ago who ganged up and killed a man to claim his estate and beautiful daughters. A curse came on them, and he said today, those families are almost extinct.

4) Immorality and Fornication: 1 Corinthians 6:18-20 says,

> *"Flee from sexual immorality. All other sins a person commits are outside the body, but whoever sins sexually,*

sins against their own body. Do you not know that your bodies are temples of the Holy Spirit, who is in you, whom you have received from God? You are not your own; you were bought at a price. Therefore, honor God with your bodies."

King David committed adultery with Bathsheba and had her husband Uriah killed. As a result, his family was cursed, and his son Absalom murdered his brother Amnon. A lot went wrong in his family.

Some diseases that are eating up some families came through adultery committed by a parent. My father told me about a man whose family was ruined because he took his brother's wife. His brother cursed him.

5) Unforgiveness and Bitterness: Matthew 6:14-15 says,

"For if you forgive other people when they sin against you, your heavenly Father will also forgive you. But if you do not forgive others their sins, your Father will not forgive your sins."

Ephesians 4:26-27 reveals that demons exploit unforgiveness to invade and destroy individuals. Esau harbored bitterness and unforgiveness towards his brother Jacob (Genesis 27:1-46). As a result, Esau's family was cursed, and his descendants became enemies of Israel.

Today, some families are suffering because of the quarrels and enmities of their ancestors.

6) Dishonoring Parents: Exodus 20:12 says,

"Honor your father and your mother, so that you may live long in the land the Lord your God is giving you."

"Cursed is anyone who dishonors their father or mother" *(Deuteronomy 27:16).*

A curse will come upon a child who dishonors their parents, and their offspring will be affected.

7) **Breaking Covenants and Vows:** Numbers 30:2 says,
"When a man makes a vow to the Lord or takes an oath to obligate himself by a pledge, he must not break his word but must do everything he said."
"Cursed is anyone who moves their neighbor's boundary stone" (Deuteronomy 27:17).

Shifting a boundary mark, breaking a business agreement, and so on bring curses.

Some people suffer because they broke their marriage vows, which affects their children.

8) **Stealing and coveting:** Exodus 20:15, 17 says,
"You shall not steal. You shall not covet anything that belongs to your neighbor."

Achan stole from the spoils of war and hid the treasure in his tent (Joshua 7:1-26). As a result, his family was cursed, and they were stoned to death. Some families are cursed because of stolen property.

9) **Murder and Bloodshed:** Genesis 9:5-6 says,
"And for your lifeblood I will surely demand an accounting. I will demand an accounting from every animal. And from each human being, too, I will demand an accounting for the life of another human being."

Cain murdered his brother Abel and was cursed (Genesis 4:1-16). Verify in your community, and you will discover that families where their fathers were executioners, slave traders, or murderers die prematurely, die through accidents or violently, or are violent.

What Has God Provided For Family Deliverance?

Here are some biblical provisions for deliverance from family curses and bondages:

1. Repentance and Confession

1 John 1:9 says,
"If we confess our sins, he is faithful and just and will forgive us our sins and purify us from all unrighteousness."

When the children of Israel decided to repent of their idolatry and return to God with all their hearts, God came down in their midst and delivered them from the Philistines. This is what Prophet Samuel told them:

> *"So Samuel said to all the Israelites, 'If you are returning to the* Lord *with all your hearts, then rid yourselves of the foreign gods and the Ashtoreths and commit yourselves to the* Lord *and serve him only, and he will deliver you out of the hand of the Philistines." So the Israelites put away their Baals and Ashtoreths, and served the* Lord *only"* (1 Sam. 7:3-4).

If you want God to deliver your family from demonic harassments, repent from idolatry, burn the idols (Deuteronomy 7:1-4), and serve Him alone.

Unfortunately, people want deliverance and prosperity without repentance. If you give money to anyone to deliver your family from curses and evil foundations, and you don't repent and throw away your idol, you are wasting precious time and your hard-earned money.

2. Forgiveness

Matthew 6:14-15 says,

> *"For if you forgive other people when they sin against you, your heavenly Father will also forgive you. But if you do not forgive others their sins, your Father will not forgive your sins."*

God wants to forgive us, both as individuals and as families. We must also be willing to forgive and let go of our hurts. Joseph forgave his brothers who had sold him and restored his family (Genesis 45:1-15).

Do you want your family to be free from curses and evil foundations? Forgive those who have hurt you from your heart. I followed a Church member to a village in Mbouda for his father's burial. I noticed that their neighbors in the village were not concerned about what was happening in the deceased's compound. When I asked why, he told me their parents had been enemies for over fifty years, and the two families do not greet each other. Maybe your family has a similar situation. Please do something about it.

3. Redemption through the Blood of Christ

Galatians 3:13-14 says,

> *"Christ redeemed us from the curse of the law by becoming a curse for us, for it is written: 'Cursed is everyone who is hung on a pole.' He redeemed us in order that the blessing given to Abraham might come to the Gentiles through Christ Jesus, so that by faith we might receive the promise of the Spirit."*

The purpose of a curse is to destroy. Jesus took your curses on the cross and was crucified. He died for you. Come to Him and receive freedom by faith. As soon as you surrender to Jesus Christ and decide to follow Him as His disciple, every curse in your life loses its legal ground.

It is based on the finished work of the cross – the price paid for you, that you can boldly claim your freedom by the blood of Jesus Christ. He became a curse for you and died. Why must you die again? A debt is paid once. Jesus has paid it for you, once and for all. Why must you carry the curse He took upon Himself on the cross? To accept demons to torment you with curses is equal to saying that Jesus died in vain. God forbids it!

4. Spiritual Warfare

> *"And these signs will accompany those who believe: in my name they will cast out demons" (Mark 16:17).*
>
> *"Jesus called his twelve disciples together and gave them authority to cast out evil spirits and to heal every kind of disease and illness" (Matthew 10:1).*
>
> *"However, this kind does not go out except by prayer and fasting" (Matthew 17:21).*

After you have surrendered to Christ and repented of your sins (Turn away from them), you engage in spiritual warfare against the powers of darkness. It may require fasting. Take time to fast and deal with the evil powers.

As you do warfare, angelic spirits will assist you (Hebrews 1:14).

5. The anointing of the Holy Spirit: Acts 1:8 says,

> "*But you will receive power when the Holy Spirit comes on you; and you will be my witnesses in Jerusalem, and in all Judea and Samaria, and to the ends of the earth.*"
>
> "*And it shall come to pass in that day, that his burden shall be taken away from off thy shoulder, and his yoke from off thy neck, and the yoke shall be destroyed because of the anointing*" *(Isaiah 10:27).*

God has given us the anointing to destroy the works of Satan. At this point, seek ministration from anointed servants of God if you cannot deal with the situation.

6. Divine restoration: The Bible in Joel 2:25-26 says,

> "*I will repay you for the years the locusts have eaten—the great locust and the young locust, the other locusts and the locust swarm—my great army that I sent among you. You will have plenty to eat, until you are full, and you will praise the name of the Lord your God, who has worked wonders for you; never again will my people be shamed.*"

God has made provisions to restore what we lost after deliverance. After Job was delivered, God restored everything to him double (Job 42:10-17).

Steps To Family Deliverance

Here is a general guide to follow to break curses, bondages, evil altars, and conduct family deliverance:

Preparation:

1) Collect information: Some people call this spiritual mapping. Research your family history, including past traumas, sins, and strongholds. This will help you identify the issues you will be dealing with and how to pray. Get a copy of our book *Personal and Family Deliverance*. It will guide you on this.

2) Pray and fast: Before you go for deliverance, spend time in prayer and fasting to seek God's guidance, wisdom, and power. The person leading the program will decide how the fast should be done.

3) Mobilize the family: Begin with those who are saved and consecrated to Jesus Christ. After you have prayed with them, share the idea with the others. Some may not see the need to hand the family over to God because they benefit from the idolatry going on in the family. Some family heads fear losing control over family members if they become dedicated Christians.

Steps to family deliverance:
Follow these steps during the prayer session.
1) Repent and confess your sins: Lead your family to repent and confess their sins, including those of past generations (Leviticus 26:40-42, 1 John 1:9).

2) Forgiveness: Encourage family members to forgive themselves and others, releasing bitterness or resentment (Matthew 6:14-15). Ensure this is done before proceeding.

3) Renunciation: Have family members renounce any involvement with occult practices, freemasonry, or other organizations that may be contributing to bondage.

4) Burn satanic objects: Destroy all satanic objects and idols in your keeping. It is not enough to pray and raise altars. You must destroy the idols (Deuteronomy 7:1-4).

5) Break curses: Pray to break any curses you have identified that are affecting your family (Galatians 3:13-14 and Deuteronomy 21:23)

6) Anointing and prayer: You may anoint family members with oil and pray for their deliverance and healing, using scriptures like James 5:14-15 and Mark 6:13.

7) Spiritual warfare: Engage in spiritual warfare, praying against any demonic strongholds affecting your family (Ephesians 6:10-20).

8) Restoration and healing: Pray for restoration and healing in areas where your family is experiencing bondage or pain (Joel 2:25-26).

9) Raise a family altar: (For steps to raise a family altar, read my books; *Raise An Altar* and *Family Restoration 1.* For orders, contact +237 681722404)

Take Action Now!
Have you discovered through this that your family is in bondage? Don't run around and start looking for a prophet to deliver you. Settle in now and follow the instructions in this book meticulously.

Don't tell me, "I lack spiritual power or authority." I was a young believer in 1994 when I led my family to battle. I didn't count my years in the faith, nor did I trust in my own strength. I was so burdened to see my family liberated that I didn't care about what the devil was saying. Don't remain silent while your family continues to suffer. Rise and take action now. Begin the fight, and God will support you.

PRAYER POINTS
Thanksgiving:
1. *Father, thank You for redeeming us through the blood of Jesus from every curse of the law, in Jesus' name.*
2. *Lord, I thank You for giving us authority over serpents, scorpions, and all the power of the enemy, in Jesus' name.*
3. *Thank You for the testimonies of deliverance and restoration You have already performed in families, in Jesus' name.*
4. *Father, I thank You for the promise that the blessing of Abraham belongs to us through Christ Jesus, in Jesus' name.*

Repentance and Confession:
5. *Father, forgive us for every sin that has opened doors to family bondages, in Jesus' name.*

6. *Lord, we repent of idolatry, false worship, and reliance on demonic altars in our family, in Jesus' name.*

7. *Father, forgive us for injustice, oppression, and bloodshed committed by our ancestors, in Jesus' name.*

8. *Lord, have mercy on us for immorality, broken vows, and dishonor to parents that have brought curses, in Jesus' name.*

9. *Father, cleanse our family with the blood of Jesus from every hidden sin that gave the enemy legal ground, in Jesus' name.*

Breaking Evil Foundations:

10. *Every evil foundation of poverty and stagnation in my family, be destroyed by fire, in Jesus' name.*

11. *I break every curse of premature death and untimely tragedies in my household, in Jesus' name.*

12. *Lord, dismantle every altar of idolatry and witchcraft speaking against my family, in Jesus' name.*

13. *By the blood of Jesus, I break every inherited curse from my father's and mother's house, in Jesus' name.*

14. *Every strongman enforcing evil foundations in my lineage, be overthrown now, in Jesus' name.*

15. *Lord, uproot every demonic seed sown into my family foundation, in Jesus' name.*

16. *I declare that every covenant with death and destruction in my lineage is nullified, in Jesus' name.*

Deliverance from Symptoms of Bondage:

17. *Lord, break the cycle of marital failure and divorce in my family, in Jesus' name.*

18. *Father, destroy every generational pattern of barrenness and unfruitfulness, in Jesus' name.*

19. *Lord, break the chains of addictions, irresponsibility, and indebtedness in our household, in Jesus' name.*

20. *Father, cancel every generational pattern of failure at the edge of success in our family, in Jesus' name.*

21. *I break the curse of chronic sicknesses and hereditary diseases in my family line, in Jesus' name.*

22. *Lord, stop every recurring tragedy, accident, or untimely death in our household, in Jesus' name.*

Spiritual Warfare:

23. *O Lord, God of vengeance, arise and shine forth in my life. Scatter every enemy of righteousness, in Jesus' name.*

24. *Judge of the earth, rise up and repay the proud for their wickedness against me, in Jesus' name.*

25. *Let every voice of the wicked boasting against me be silenced by Your judgment, in Jesus' name.*

26. *O Lord, those who oppress and afflict Your people — let their wickedness come to a full end, in Jesus' name.*

27. *Father, every power that seeks to kill, steal, or destroy the helpless — arise and judge them, in Jesus' name.*

28. *Lord, expose every evildoer who thinks You do not see; reveal Your power in the camp of the wicked, in Jesus' name.*

29. *Every fool that mocks Your justice in my life — let divine wisdom and judgment silence them, in Jesus' name.*

30. *He who made the ear and the eye — arise and hear our cry; see our affliction and avenge us, in Jesus' name.*

31. *Let every wicked structure and law framed against the righteous be overturned by Your power, in Jesus' name.*

32. *Father, let justice return to the righteous and let the upright in heart rejoice again, in Jesus' name.*

33. *I release the fire of God to consume every serpent and dragon harassing my family, in Jesus' name.*

34. *Every demonic gatekeeper blocking my family's progress, be removed by fire, in Jesus' name.*

35. *I silence every evil voice crying against my family at demonic altars, in Jesus' name.*

36. *I command every monitoring spirit following my family to be blinded, in Jesus' name.*

37. *By the authority of Christ, I trample on every scorpion and serpent assigned against my lineage, in Jesus' name.*

38. *I declare war against ancestral spirits enforcing family curses, in Jesus' name.*

Forgiveness and Healing:

39. *Father, give us grace to forgive one another and break the cycle of bitterness, in Jesus' name.*

40. *Lord, heal every wound and restore broken family relationships, in Jesus' name.*
41. *Father, replace generational hatred with generational love and unity, in Jesus' name.*
42. *Lord, restore peace where quarrels, divisions, and enmities have reigned in our family, in Jesus' name.*
43. *By the blood of Jesus, I nullify every curse working against my family, in Jesus' name.*
44. *Let the blood of Jesus silence every accusation against our family, in Jesus' name.*
45. *By the blood of Jesus, we reclaim every blessing stolen from our family, in Jesus' name.*
46. *We declare that the blood of Jesus has redeemed our family from every bondage, in Jesus' name.*

Restoration and New Foundations:

47. *Father, restore everything that the enemy has stolen from our family, in Jesus' name.*
48. *Father, let the years wasted by curses and bondages be restored in double measure, in Jesus' name.*
49. *Lord, establish a new foundation of righteousness and blessing in our family, in Jesus' name.*
50. *May our children and future generations walk in freedom and blessing, in Jesus' name.*

Chapter 7
Days 19-21

Cultivate Perseverance

*"We do not want you to become lazy, but to imitate those who
through faith and patience inherit what has been promised"
(Hebrews 6:12 NIV)*

Perseverance is more than grit or resilience; it is a spiritual force that sustains a family through trials, transitions, and triumphs. In a world of instant gratification and impulsive decisions, a family that would endure and thrive must be grounded in faith-filled perseverance.

Impatience, instant gratification, and a shortcut mentality have destroyed many families. God desires your family to walk in His blessing, but that blessing comes through a process, not a quick fix or one instant miracle. Sadly, many people want the product but not the process. How can you arrive at your destination without making the journey?

To truly receive what God has ordained, you must go through the process – walk with Him in patience and faith. Shortcuts will never lead you to His perfect plan for you. Lasting blessings take time, trust, and spiritual endurance. If you're willing, God will strengthen you and help you develop the capacity to persevere. With Him, your family can overcome delays and disappointments, moving forward into everything He has prepared for you, step by step, season by season.

It takes time to build a great family. In fact, each admirable family has a story of ups and downs. But God's grace takes them higher as they follow Him patiently. Change the way you interpret setbacks in your family, and things will change.

An Invitation to America

In August 2000, a breakthrough message came through the radio: my mother, a dedicated rural women's leader from Lebialem Division in Cameroon's South West Region, had been selected to represent rural Cameroonian women in a program at the United Nations Headquarters in New York. What a divine visitation! Joy exploded in our family. "Finally," we thought, "Someone from our family is going to America. Praise God!"

At the time, she was in Bafang, helping my wife with our newborn son. But with this news, she rushed to Buea to start the travel process. Despite financial hardship, she miraculously secured the first passport in our family and applied for the U.S. visa alongside other women leaders invited for the UN program.

To our amazement, the US Embassy granted a six-month visa, twice the duration given to the other women. However, there was a painful twist. She needed 700,000 FCFA (about $1,000) to buy her plane ticket, and we simply couldn't raise it. Though the inviting organization promised to reimburse participants, that didn't help us to obtain a loan for her. Every door we knocked on stayed shut. Eventually, the other women traveled and returned. My mother stayed behind, visa in hand, heartbroken.

Some friends whispered, "Sell the visa."

She told me about it.

"No, Mama," I said firmly. "Don't sell it. I'll frame it and hang it on my wall. One day I'll tell your grandchildren, 'Your grandmother had a visa to America, but poverty kept her from going.'"

She returned to our village, Bamumbu, and life continued. But about a month before the visa expired, a man who worked in the

Divisional Office and often ate in our home asked about her trip. Shocked that she hadn't traveled, he offered her a loan of 500,000 FCFA (about $700).

She accepted it. But another problem arose: who would receive her in America? After much searching, someone connected her to a woman in Maryland who needed help with her children. My mother embraced the opportunity and flew out.

Weeks later, I received a call from a call box. "It's me, pastor," she said. "I'm in America, and everything is moving well." You cannot imagine the joy that filled my heart.

Later, she called again and said, "They say I should apply for asylum so that I can bring you and your siblings over."

I paused, then told her, "Mama, don't lie to stay in America. Come back. God will make another way."

She submitted to the counsel, canceling the process and losing $500 in legal fees. But she gained something priceless, integrity.

When she returned, I prophesied to her, "You'll go again."

Two weeks later, another invitation came, and in July 2002, she returned to the U.S., this time with my younger brother, who had been admitted to the University of Dallas, Texas.

Due to overstaying during her first visit, the U.S. Embassy later denied her travel for years. But in 2025, she finally traveled again, with her husband, and both received green cards.

That same green card that the enemy once tempted her to obtain through deceit, God gave it to her freely, in His time.

Today, fifteen family members are in the U.S., three in Canada, and the doors of nations have opened to our household. By God's grace, I am writing this story from Belgium, having visited the U.S. and France. This isn't boasting. It's a testimony. We followed the hard and patient path and reaped lasting blessings. That's the power of perseverance, obedience, and integrity. It is worth emulating!

The Way Will Be Difficult

My early days were painfully hard. I didn't know then that I was enrolled in God's training academy. It became clear later that God was shaping me for something greater.

One night in 1995, while studying at the Full Gospel Bible Institute (FGBI), I sat quietly on my bed in the dormitory, silently sobbing. I cried and asked God, "Why have You forgotten me?" I eventually fell asleep and had a dream that marked me for life.

In the dream, I stood outside the dormitory with classmates. We saw a large plantain tree with a huge immature bunch. They tried harvesting it with bamboos. As I stepped forward to do the same, a voice said, *"Don't! Wait for it to be ready."* I stopped. Suddenly, I was on the school football field, looking at a massive mango tree full of unripe fruits. Again, my friends tried to harvest them. The voice repeated, *"Don't! Wait for the fruits to be ripe. When the time comes, just shake the branches and gather as many as you want."*

When I woke up, I heard God say, *"Your beginning will be hard, but your end will be glorious."* That word has anchored me through many storms in ministry. Even now, I hear it in my spirit: *"Keep going, your end will be glorious."* The way with God may be difficult, but the end is always glorious.

When we first come to Christ, God often paints a prophetic picture of our destiny. If you're spiritually alert, you can glimpse it, often through dreams, visions, or inner impressions. These early revelations are like divine blueprints meant to anchor your faith and guide your life's journey. Stay vigilant, God will speak to you.

This is Your Portion

In 1997, while on my first pastoral assignment in Bafang, I went on a one-week fasting and prayer retreat. Each day, I rose early to seek God, reading Scripture, meditating, and praying from morning till evening. One afternoon, I was reading through the book of Joshua, particularly the chapters that describe how the Promised Land was divided among the tribes of Israel. After reading for some time, I paused and asked, *"Father, what does this have to do with me? What is my portion in all this?"* To my surprise, I heard a clear, audible voice: *"Your portion is in Isaiah 54."*

I quickly turned to the chapter. As I read, the words aligned exactly with a dream I'd had two years earlier, in which God said: *"Your beginning will be barren, but your end will be abundantly fruitful."*

Since that day, Isaiah 54 has become the foundation of my life and ministry. From it, I have received my message, mandate, and mantle for restoration for my ministry. Year after year, I've patiently watched the promises in Isaiah 54 unfold with precision, confirming that it was indeed my prophetic portion. Just as Isaiah 61 was the life scripture for Jesus, Isaiah 54 has been mine.

Your portion in Christ will come through a process. Be willing to follow the Lord faithfully, patiently, and courageously.

What is Perseverance?

The Old Testament word "Perseverance" is translated from the Hebrew *'qavah,'* which means "To wait eagerly or to hope expectantly," as seen in Isaiah 40:31: ***"They who wait for the Lord shall renew their strength."*** So, perseverance includes hopeful waiting.

In the New Testament, "Perseverance" is translated from the Greek *'hypomone,'* which means "Endurance, steadfastness, patient continuance, or holding up under pressure." It is rooted in the idea of remaining under a heavy burden without giving up.

Practically, perseverance is the steadfast and patient endurance to continue doing what is right and trusting God, even when it is hard, delayed, or painful. It is the inner strength to remain faithful despite obstacles, suffering, or discouragement.

Perseverance serves as a solid foundation for family blessing:

- ***"We can rejoice, too, when we run into problems and trials, for we know that they help us develop endurance. And endurance develops strength of character, and character strengthens our confident hope of salvation" (Romans 5:3-4 NLT).***

Trials are God's training ground for perseverance, which leads to spiritual maturity and hope.

- ***"God blesses those who patiently endure testing and temptation. Afterward, they will receive the crown of life that God has promised to those who love him" (James 1:12 NLT).***

Endurance through testing leads to reward and blessing.

- *"Patient endurance is what you need now, so that you will continue to do God's will. Then you will receive all that he has promised" (Hebrews 10:36 NLT).*

Perseverance is the bridge between obedience and fulfilled promise.

Trials don't break a blessed family; they refine it. Patience and faithfulness build spiritual endurance and godly character in them.

God's Promises Take Time

"We do not want you to become lazy, but to imitate those who through faith and patience inherit what has been promised" (Hebrews 6:12 NIV)

God's promises take time. However, you must embrace the process. This verse is part of an exhortation to believers who were growing weary and considering giving up their faith in Christ. The writer of Hebrews warns them against spiritual passivity and urges them to imitate the faith and patience of the patriarchs, especially Abraham (see verses 13-15), who received God's promise of a great family and a future after years of delay and struggle.

Abraham is a model of a believer who faithfully and patiently followed and served God until he received his promises. Without a pastor to follow him up, a church community to support him, or a Bible to guide him, Abraham served God and became the father of faith. We have to follow his example.

Abraham's family carried a divine promise:

"I will make you into a great nation" (Genesis 12:2).

Yet, that promise didn't come to pass instantly. In fact, it unfolded over multiple generations and through much struggle. Abraham and Sarah battled barrenness for 25 years before Isaac was born (Genesis 21:5). But the pattern didn't end there. Isaac and Rebekah also struggled with infertility for 20 years before Jacob and Esau were born (Genesis 25:20-26). Then Jacob's beloved wife, Rachel, waited several years, at least 7 to 14 years into her marriage, before Joseph was finally born (Genesis 30:22-24).

Through these delays, God was working out His purposes in Abraham's family. It wasn't just about having children; it was about raising a lineage of faith that could steward the blessing. Once Joseph was born, the tide turned. Through him, the Israelites were brought into

Egypt, and there they multiplied exceedingly (Exodus 1:7). However, from Abraham to the birth of Moses, who led Israel out of Egypt, approximately 500 years had passed.

The lesson to be learned from this is that God's promises are sure, but they are not always immediate. They unfold over time and through testing. Some of the most glamorous promises God has made to your family may require you to endure a season or seasons of barrenness before you see fruitfulness.

If you succumb to impatience, you may introduce a wrong foundation in your family. Sarah, in a moment of impatience, introduced Hagar to Abraham, a culturally acceptable but spiritually damaging decision (Genesis 16:1-4). Ishmael was born, but he was not the son of promise. That act of compromise introduced generational tension between the Jews and the Arabs that still affects the world today.

Faith without patience leads to fleshly decisions. Don't settle for an Ishmael when God has promised you an Isaac. No matter the pressure, wait on God for things to unfold at the right time.

"He has made everything beautiful in its time" (Ecclesiastes 3:11).

Blessings are wonderful and lasting only when they come at the right time. Mangoes are good, but terrible when you harvest them before their time. A car is good, but you may need to borrow money to buy fuel for it if you got it at the wrong time. Everything must be done at the right time. Wait for God's time!

Biblical Families Blessed Through Perseverance

The Bible is filled with examples of men and women who, through unwavering perseverance, led their families to divine blessings and made a lasting generational impact. They didn't give up in trials, delay, or disappointment. Instead, they endured with faith, obeyed God in difficult seasons, and became instruments of supernatural breakthrough for their households. Let us consider three of these remarkable individuals:

1. Noah's Family – *Saved through persevering obedience*

Noah's family was preserved not by chance, but through decades of persevering obedience. Though warned of a flood no one had ever seen,

Noah built the ark as God commanded, despite mockery and delay (Genesis 6:22). He labored for 120 years to accomplish the project. His unwavering obedience and perseverance became the ark of salvation for his entire household.

> **"By faith Noah... built an ark to save his family" (Hebrews 11:7 NLT).**

In a world of compromise, he stood firm. Because he persisted, his family was spared from judgment (Genesis 7:1).

Are you living in obedience, yet still facing overwhelming challenges? Let Noah's example remind you: faithful obedience may take time, but it secures lasting results for generations. Don't become weary in doing God's will; your family will be blessed.

2. Job – *Perseverance that restores a family*

Job's story is one of the Bible's most explicit pictures of perseverance in the face of unimaginable loss. In one season, he lost his children, wealth, health, and reputation. Even his wife urged him to curse God and die (Job 2:9). Yet Job held on to his integrity and refused to abandon his faith.

Though confused, heartbroken, and physically devastated, Job never stopped revering God. The Bible says,

> **Then Job arose and tore his robe and shaved his head and fell on the ground and worshiped. And he said, "Naked I came from my mother's womb, and naked shall I return. The Lord gave, and the Lord has taken away; blessed be the name of the Lord. In all this Job did not sin or charge God with wrong" (Job 1:20-22).**

His perseverance wasn't perfect, but it was steadfast. He didn't walk away from the faith, even when God seemed silent.

Job 42 reveals the result of that perseverance: God restored him and gave him double what he had lost. His daughters were honored, and his family line was preserved. Job's perseverance didn't just redeem him; it restored his household and became a generational testimony. His story is a blessing to us today.

Is your family facing loss and failure? Learn from Job. Your perseverance in faith and obedience to God will deliver and restore you.

God's power will move and open the door to supernatural restoration, in Jesus' name.

3. Zechariah and Elizabeth – *Perseverance that births a prophetic destiny*

They were described as

"…righteous before God, walking in all the commandments and ordinances of the Lord blameless" (Luke 1:6).

Yet, they suffered the pain of childlessness into old age, a condition often misunderstood as divine disapproval – a curse. Still, they persevered in faith and obedience, never abandoning their service to God.

At the appointed time, God answered them:

"Do not be afraid, Zacharias… your prayer is heard" (Luke 1:13).

Elizabeth conceived and gave birth to John the Baptist, the prophet who would

"go before the Lord to prepare His ways" (Luke 1:76).

Their years of faithfulness resulted in a child with a prophetic assignment, impacting all of Israel and preparing the world for Christ.

Has God's prophecy concerning you or your family been delayed, and you feel like giving up? The perseverance of this couple teaches us that waiting in faith positions us for generational impact. God is preparing something big through you. His promises in your life are not bound by age or delay; they will be fulfilled in His perfect timing. Persevere!

Families Destroyed Through Impatience & Hasty Schemes

Several families in the Bible were torn apart by impatience and quick schemes. Instead of trusting God's timing and plan, they took matters into their own hands, with painful consequences. When you take matters into your own hands instead of submitting to God's plan, you risk handing your destiny over to the torment of the enemy.

1. Isaac's Family – *When impatience divides a family*

The family of Isaac and Rebekah is a sobering lesson on how impatience and manipulation can fracture a household. Impatience almost ruined their family. The Bible says,

"Rebekah took the best clothes of Esau... and put them on her younger son Jacob" (Genesis 27:15 NIV).

God had already spoken to Rebecca that the older son, Esau, would serve the younger, Jacob (Genesis 25:23). Yet instead of waiting for God's word to unfold, Rebekah devised a deceitful plan to secure the blessing. Jacob, influenced by his mother, tricked his aging father. Esau, feeling robbed of the blessing and bitter, vowed to kill his brother (Genesis 27:41). The result was a family torn apart by schemes rooted in impatience and favoritism.

Though Jacob was part of God's plan, the method used to advance his destiny left scars of betrayal, division, and decades of separation. God's purposes do not need human manipulation. You should not try to help God through ungodly schemes like the unbelievers. Has God promised you that you will travel abroad? You don't need to lie to make it happen. You don't need to devise crooked plans like an unbeliever to prosper financially.

Friend, as a family, if you take shortcuts, you will prolong your suffering. But if you persevere, God will surely bless you with lasting blessings. His promises are best fulfilled His way, in His time.

2. Ananias' Family – *When greed destroys a household*

Ananias and Sapphira were part of the early Church's revival atmosphere. But instead of walking in transparency, they chose deceit. In a rush to gain recognition like others who had given sacrificially, they sold a property and conspired to lie about the amount. Peter asked them,

"How could you agree to test the Spirit of the Lord?" (Acts 5:9 NIV).

Their hasty scheme wasn't just about money; it was about the appearance of devotion without true obedience. That is hypocrisy. Both were struck dead for lying to the Holy Spirit (Acts 5:3-10).

The judgment of Ananias and Saphira is a sobering warning to us today that greed and hypocrisy can destroy not just an individual but their entire family. Devising schemes to appear blessed, successful, or sacrificial without integrity is deadly.

God desires truth in our inward parts (Psalm 51:6). Are you pressured to take a shortcut to obtain a breakthrough? Don't succumb; it will trap your destiny. It's better to wait, obey, and walk in the light than to rush into schemes that invite judgment. Proverbs 15:16 counsels,

"Better to be poor and fear the Lord than to be rich and in trouble."

Somebody said, "The road to ruin is paved with spiritual shortcuts."

How to Cultivate a Mindset of Perseverance

Creating a family culture of perseverance isn't just about navigating through tough seasons; it's about establishing your family deeply in faith, vision, and disciplined habits that lead to lasting blessings.

You are aware that human nature, especially in today's generation, craves quick results, often with little regard for the means to obtain them. But if you're determined to walk closely with God and experience lasting blessings, you must learn the art of perseverance. Let's explore four foundational principles that will help you cultivate a mindset of perseverance within your family.

1. Set Your Mind on God's Promises for Your Family

The starting point for perseverance is vision. Hebrews 12:2 tells us that Jesus endured the cross *"for the joy set before Him."* Likewise, your family must be rooted in God's promises, eternal joy, peace, provision, and legacy. When your mind is fixed on God's truth, temporary obstacles lose their power. Consider Abraham, who hoped against hope because he trusted God's covenant (Romans 4:18-21).

Families grounded in Scripture develop deep resilience. In 1988, my father returned from a retreat carrying a chart with a verse boldly printed at the top:

"Behold, I and the children whom the Lord has given me are for signs and wonders" (Isaiah 8:18).

He stood before us and declared, "This is our family verse." That same chart still hangs in our home today. Since then, he has prayed this Scripture over us thousands of times. To this day, if you ask any of his children or grandchildren about our family verse, they'll immediately say, "Isaiah 8:18."

Hearing that verse repeatedly shaped our identity, clarified our vision, and fueled our commitment to follow God's plan. You can do the same. Post God's promises visibly, pray them aloud, and weave them into daily conversations. William Damon, a leading expert in adolescent development, found that children with a strong sense of purpose are more persistent and emotionally resilient. When you speak purpose over your family, anchoring it in God's Word, you lay the foundation for lasting perseverance, which establishes you in God's blessings.

2. Stick to the Plan

God does everything with a clear plan, and He has one for your family's blessing. Even when it gets hard, don't deviate from the path God has laid out for your family. Jesus consistently followed His Father's will, even when it meant suffering (Luke 22:42). Many people start well but quit when things get uncomfortable. But perseverance requires a steady commitment to what God has already spoken.

Jeremiah 29:11 says,

"For I know the plans I have for you… plans to prosper you and not to harm you." Strategic planning is key to success. Years ago, I saw others advancing while I had nothing. I prayed, and God showed me that I needed a plan. With a small salary, He led me to buy affordable plots of land to sell later and raise money to build our family home. That strategy worked, and today we have a house. It took us about 13 years to get there. God gave us something far better than what my colleague got long ago.

I've learned that every major goal, especially in family life, requires prayerful planning. Sit with God, write down His strategy, and stick to it. Your family will thrive through it.

3. Build a Culture of Prayer

Prayer isn't just a spiritual routine; it is the heartbeat of a persevering family. It was central to Jesus' life and ministry (Luke 5:16). Through fervent prayer in Gethsemane (Matthew 26:36-46; Luke 22:39-46), He developed the strength to endure the cross.

When prayer becomes a consistent habit in your home, it fosters emotional stability, spiritual sensitivity, and deep trust in God. Studies show that families who pray together regularly experience greater peace, unity, and emotional support.

Make prayer part of your family's daily rhythm – before meals, during decisions, and in hard moments. Let your children see you pray through struggles and praise through victories. I cannot forget the series of fasting programs my father organized to pray for a new job when he was unemployed. We were young, but his commitment to seeking God left a strong impression on us. He finally got a breakthrough. I learned from him to seek God when facing challenges.

In 1995, we raised a prophetic prayer altar in our family. We gathered to pray for healing, guidance, and breakthrough. God has done so much through that altar. Today, with social media and video calls, it's even easier to create a virtual family altar where you pray and minister to one another. A family that prays together builds unshakable bonds, stands stronger in adversity, and walks together in victory.

4. Learn from Other People of Faith

We're not meant to walk this journey alone. Hebrews 12:1 reminds us that a great cloud of witnesses surrounds us – those who've gone before us in faith. Learning from the testimonies of others cultivates our hope and strengthens perseverance.

Share biographies of faith heroes with your family members. I have shared the stories of some families that enjoyed God's blessings through perseverance and those who crumbled because of get-rich-quick schemes. You can research and read more about them. The knowledge acquired will strengthen your faith and help you remain steadfast.

Studies show that storytelling increases empathy and resilience in children. Invite spiritual mentors into your family's life, listen to faith-building podcasts, and attend church regularly. We read books together as a family, and learning from the stories of other families has been very helpful. As Jim Rohn said, "You are the average of the five people you spend the most time with." Surround your family with faith-filled examples and watch perseverance grow.

Stay on the Course

Perseverance is the bridge between vision and fulfillment, process and promise. It is the divine force that strengthens families to endure hardship, wait with faith, and walk with God through trials to triumph and blessings. While shortcuts may offer temporary solutions, only endurance leads to lasting blessings.

Just as Noah, Job, and Elizabeth persevered and saw God's faithfulness, your family, too, can overcome delays and disappointments through faith, patience, and obedience. Never trade integrity for quick results. Stay on the course, cling to God's Word, and you'll see fruit in due season. Perseverance doesn't just shape destiny; it secures it for generational blessings.

PRAYER POINTS

Thanksgiving:

1. *Father, thank You for the gift of perseverance that sustains families through trials, in Jesus' name.*
2. *Thank You, Lord, for every testimony of endurance that has preserved blessings in our family, in Jesus' name.*
3. *Father, we thank You for the promises of Scripture that give us hope to endure, in Jesus' name.*
4. *Thank You for the examples of biblical families who inherited blessings through faith and patience, in Jesus' name.*

Repentance and Renewal:

5. *Lord, forgive us for impatience and seeking shortcuts instead of waiting on You, in Jesus' name.*
6. *Father, forgive us for murmuring and doubting during seasons of delay, in Jesus' name.*
7. *Lord, cleanse our family from every decision made out of compromise and fleshly impatience, in Jesus' name.*
8. *Father, renew in us the strength to endure trials faithfully until Your promises are fulfilled, in Jesus' name.*

Strength to Persevere:

9. *Father, give my family supernatural strength to endure hardships, in Jesus' name.*

10. *Lord, help us to wait patiently for Your timing in all things, in Jesus' name.*

11. *May we persevere in obedience even when mocked or misunderstood, in Jesus' name.*

12. *Lord, teach us to interpret setbacks as stepping stones to blessings, in Jesus' name.*

13. *Father, give us faith that refuses to give up, in Jesus' name.*

14. *Lord, sustain us with fresh oil when our strength is failing, in Jesus' name.*

Faith in God's Promises:

15. *Father, anchor our family in the promises of Your Word, in Jesus' name.*

16. *Lord, may the vision of Your promises keep us steadfast in trials, in Jesus' name.*

17. *Father, help us to hold on like Abraham until every promise is fulfilled, in Jesus' name.*

18. *Lord, may we never settle for Ishmael when You have promised us Isaac, in Jesus' name.*

19. *Father, give us patience to receive every blessing at its appointed time, in Jesus' name.*

Victory Over Impatience and Schemes:

20. *Lord, deliver us from the spirit of impatience and compromise, in Jesus' name.*

21. *Father, break the cycle of fleshly decisions that cause generational pain, in Jesus' name.*

22. *Lord, let us never trade integrity for quick solutions, in Jesus' name.*

23. *Father, expose every trap of the enemy designed to lure us into shortcuts, in Jesus' name.*

24. *Lord, deliver our children from the desire for instant gratification, in Jesus' name.*

Endurance Through Trials:

25. *Lord, help us to stand firm in faith like Job in the face of loss, in Jesus' name.*

26. *Father, give us the endurance of Noah to obey You even when it takes years, in Jesus' name.*

27. *Lord, help us persevere in prayer like Zechariah and Elizabeth until our promise is birthed, in Jesus' name.*

28. *Father, let our perseverance refine our character and strengthen our faith, in Jesus' name.*

29. *Lord, may every trial we face become a testimony of endurance for future generations, in Jesus' name.*

30. *Father, crown our perseverance with lasting blessings, in Jesus' name.*

Destroying Spiritual Parasites:

31. *Father, let Your blood disinfect my life from every demonic parasite, in Jesus' name.*
32. *Fire of God, fall and consume every parasite tormenting my soul, in Jesus' name.*
33. *Let every parasite of lust and immorality be burned to ashes, in Jesus' name.*
34. *Mighty finger of God, enter my body and flush out invisible satanic parasites, in Jesus' name.*
35. *I purge every demonic deposit from my system by the living water of Christ, in Jesus' name.*
36. *Every parasite draining my strength and peace, be uprooted now, in Jesus' name.*
37. *Every parasite attacking my womb and fertility, be destroyed, in Jesus' name.*
38. *Garments of spiritual parasites on my body, catch fire and burn, in Jesus' name.*
39. *You parasite, placing cobwebs on my face, catch fire, in Jesus' name.*
40. *Every parasite making people reject or fear me, be removed, in Jesus' name.*
41. *Parasites projecting false images of me to others, die now, in Jesus' name.*
42. *Angel of purification, terminate every parasitic work in my life, in Jesus' name.*
43. *Every human parasite assigned to destroy me, be exposed and expelled, in Jesus' name.*
44. *Father, vaccinate me and my family against spiritual parasites this year, in Jesus' name.*

Restoration and Fruitfulness:

45. *Father, restore everything lost through impatience in our family, in Jesus' name.*
46. *Lord, make every barren season in our family fruitful in Your time, in Jesus' name.*
47. *Father, turn every delay into a testimony of Your faithfulness, in Jesus' name.*
48. *Lord, let perseverance in our family open doors to generational increase, in Jesus' name.*
49. *Father, establish our family as a testimony of waiting faithfully on You, in Jesus' name.*
50. *We prophesy that every promise of God to our family will manifest in due season, in Jesus' name.*

Chapter 8
Days 22-24

Sacrificial Love

"... Love bears all things, believes all things, hopes all things, endures all things. Love never ends" (1 Corinthians 13:7-8).

Love is a family builder. A passion for God and compassion for one another are vital capital for raising a blessed family. Your family can't flourish when there are tensions, divisions, accusations, and constant conflict. You cannot build a strong family while members are at war, tearing each other down.

Many families today are stuck and frustrated because of unresolved disputes. While they fight among themselves, they often blame the devil for their misery. The truth is, no matter what else you do, without love, you will never build the family you dream about.

Do you know that if you don't live in love, you are not living in God? Life without genuine love is lifeless and defeated.

I know many families that are in deep pain because of a love deficiency. Let me underline this truth: anyone who carries anger, bitterness, self-pity, or regret is not walking in love. Such a person is enduring life rather than enjoying it. Worse of all, Satan works freely in such an environment to destroy destinies. Could it be that your marriage and family is where it is now because of the absence of God's love?

147

Love is the key. Your passion for God guarantees your portion with Him; your compassion for people secures your promotion among men. While envy, jealousy, and unhealthy competition are seeking to destroy your family, God's love will promote and preserve it. Friend, a heart for God is the key you need to take your family to great heights. Your family will become unstoppable if you intentionally get it rooted in divine love. Truly, things always work together for those who love God.

> *"And we know that all things work together for good to those who love God, to those who are the called according to His purpose" (Romans 8:28).*

And also,

> *"What no eye has seen, nor ear heard, nor the heart of man imagined, what God has prepared for those who love him" (1 Corinthians 2:9).*

God has great and unimaginable blessings reserved for your family. That is why no matter what your family is facing right now, healing and restoration will come if you choose to walk in God's love. In the following chapter, I will show you how to create an atmosphere of love in your family that will attract God's lasting blessings.

The Story of Nicky Cruz: How Love Broke the Chains

One of the stories that marked me profoundly as a teenager was that of Nicky Cruz. The criminal who became an evangelist. His story is a powerful example of how evil within a family can cripple destinies and how God's love can redeem the most broken life.

Nicky was born on December 6, 1938, in Puerto Rico, into a home plagued by darkness. His parents practiced witchcraft and filled their house with occult rituals. His mother constantly cursed, calling him "Son of Satan." Abuse, neglect, and violence created deep wounds in his heart. Without the security of love, he grew up hardened, angry, and convinced that he was unwanted.

At the age of 15, his parents sent him to live with his elder brother in New York, but soon after, he fled to the streets. There he was swallowed up by crime, drugs, and gang culture. He became the leader of the notorious "Mau Mau gang," feared for his violence and cruelty. The devil had found in him a willing instrument, and through him, many young lives were drawn into destruction.

But God had a plan. He sent a young preacher named David Wilkerson to the streets of New York. Wilkerson was not intimidated by Nicky's threats or hardened exterior. Instead, he spoke to Nicky about Jesus, and more importantly, he showed him genuine love. When Nicky threatened to kill him, David calmly replied, "You could cut me into a thousand pieces, and every piece would still love you." Those words pierced Nicky's heart. For the first time, he saw a love that was fearless, unconditional, and real – the very love he had never known in his family. That encounter broke through years of hate. Soon after, Nicky surrendered his life to Jesus Christ.

Today, Nicky Cruz is an evangelist, preaching the same love that saved him to thousands around the world. His life proves that while evil in a family can ruin destinies, a family, or even one person, filled with God's love can make a tremendous difference, raising agents of revival and transformation.

Nowadays, through Satan's influence, many families have become tragic places where great destinies are lost. Like Nicky Cruz, numerous children are growing up emotionally and psychologically devastated because those meant to love them are instead hating, abusing, and cursing them. How is your home? How is your family? There is an urgent need for God's love to fill our homes. It is the only environment where broken hearts are healed, destinies restored, and the next generation empowered to thrive in His purpose.

What is Love?

We have just seen how love became the transforming power that rebuilt the broken lives of Nicky Cruz and Pastor Nick Vujicic. But what exactly is "Love," especially when applied to the life of your family?

Many people define love in purely natural terms – as a warm feeling, emotional attraction, or the pleasure of someone's company. Some limit love to giving and receiving. While these forms of love have their place, they cannot produce the kind of family God desires for you. Natural love is often conditional, swayed by moods, personal benefit, or changing circumstances.

1 Corinthians 13:7-8 says,

"…*Love bears all things, believes all things, hopes all things, endures all things. Love never fails.*"

The love that truly builds a strong and blessed family is what the New Testament calls '*Agape,*' – the God-kind of love. This love is far greater than anything human effort can sustain. It is unconditional, meaning it is not based on how the other person behaves. It is selfless, seeking the good of others above personal comfort or benefit. It is described as divine love because it flows from God's nature in us (1 John 4:8).

Unlike '*Phileo,*' which is friendship love, or '*Eros,*' which is romantic love, *agape* is not driven by fleeting emotions. It is anchored in the will. It is a deliberate, consistent decision to love regardless of merit, faults, or circumstances. It continues to give even when it receives nothing in return. It forgives when it has every reason to resent. It sacrifices when it would be easier to walk away.

David Wilkerson relentlessly demonstrated *agape*, the unconditional love of God, to Nicky Cruz, a feared and violent gang leader. Again and again, he reached out to him, even at the risk of his own life, undeterred by threats or rejection. That unwavering love broke through Nicky's hardened heart until the day he finally surrendered his life to Jesus Christ. This is the love that heals wounds, restores trust, and creates an atmosphere where God's blessings can rest upon your family. Without *agape*, your family will crumble under pressure and be ruined by the devil. But with it, you can triumph over any storm and flourish.

In 1 Corinthians 13:8, Paul says, **"*Love never fails.*"** Let me ask you, "If God's love never fails, can you walk in divine love and end up a failure in life?" Never!

The Story of Nick Vujicic – *The Transforming Power of Love*

Love has the power to transform the worst situations into the best, and no life illustrates this better than Pastor Nick Vujicic's story. Born on December 4, 1982, in Melbourne, Australia, Nick came into the world without arms and legs due to a rare condition called tetra-amelia syndrome. From the start, he faced challenges that could have defined his life as one of limitation and despair.

Nick's parents, Bob and Lenka Vujicic, faced the reality of his condition with strength, but the difficulties of raising a child with severe disabilities created emotional distance. Nick often felt unloved and rejected, even within his own family. This pain led him into deep despair as a boy. At the age of 10, Nick attempted to drown himself in a bathtub because of the feelings of depression, worthlessness, self-hatred, and the bullying he faced. However, he stopped his suicide attempt when he realized that his family would be more burdened by his death than by his life. This experience led him to re-evaluate his life and ultimately find faith and purpose in Jesus Christ.

His parents began to love and invest much to help him fulfill his purpose. Despite the dark beginning, love began to change Nick's life. Gradually, he learned to love and accept himself, discovering his worth beyond physical limitations. His faith in God deepened, and he realized that his life had a purpose. The love from his parents, self-love, and faith sparked healing and gave him strength.

Today, Nick Vujicic is a Christian Evangelist, a powerful motivational speaker, businessman, and founder of *Life Without Limbs*, a ministry that inspires millions worldwide. Through his ministry, books, and speeches, Nick encourages people to overcome adversity and live with hope and purpose. His message is clear: no obstacle is too great when we live with faith and love.

Nick married Kanae Miyahara, whom he met during a speaking tour in Japan, on February 12, 2012. They have two boys and twin daughters. His life reflects the transformative power of love to us. His family life is a testament to the healing and joy that God's love brings, proving that even those who begin with the greatest challenges can build a future filled with happiness and fulfillment.

Financially, Nick has also been successful, with a net worth estimated in the millions of dollars, thanks to his speaking engagements, books, and business ventures. Yet, he emphasizes that true wealth lies in the lives he touches and the hope he spreads.

Nick's story teaches us an important lesson for our families and communities. Many people who are weak, broken, or different are often rejected or overlooked. The devil seeks to destroy them by isolation and neglect. But God has placed these vulnerable individuals in our lives to be loved, nurtured, and built up. Our love will turn these weaklings into giants. It will heal their broken hearts and restore their shattered spirits. Friend, no one in your family is useless. You must commit to loving those who struggle the most, helping them rise and fulfill the unique purpose God has given them.

Jacobs's Family – *Plagued by destructive vices*

The family of Jacob, later named Israel, carried one of the most powerful blessings in history. God had promised Abraham, Isaac, and Jacob that their descendants would become a great nation, and that through them, all nations would be blessed (Genesis 28:13-15). Yet, inside Jacob's home, the very atmosphere that should have been filled with love, faith, unity, and joy was poisoned by favoritism, jealousy, resentment, competition, and hatred.

Jacob openly favored Joseph, the son of his old age. He gave him a special robe, a mark of distinction (Genesis 37:3). This foundation was laid by Isaac and Rebecca, who each had a special preference for one of the twins: Esau and Jacob (Genesis 25). The robe Jacob gave Joseph, instead of inspiring unity, became a visible symbol of partiality. The Bible says,

> *"When his brothers saw that their father loved him more... they hated him and could not speak peaceably to him" (Genesis 37:4).*

Today, how many parents like Jacob, through partiality, are sowing seeds of discord among their children?

Joseph's prophetic dreams, which foretold his future leadership, stirred **envy** rather than celebration from his brothers (Genesis 37:5-8). Instead of guarding their hearts (Proverbs 4:23) and seeking God's purpose together, the brothers allowed competition to breed bitterness. Their resentment soon turned to **malice.** Seeing Joseph coming from afar, they plotted, *"Come, let us kill him"* (Genesis 37:20). Though Reuben intervened to spare his life, they still sold him to slave traders for twenty shekels of silver (Genesis 37:28). Then they lied to their father, letting him believe Joseph was dead (Genesis 37:31-35).

The consequences were devastating:

- ***Decades of grief:*** Jacob mourned bitterly for years and refused comfort (Genesis 37:34-35).
- ***Guilt and fear:*** The brothers carried a burden of guilt, admitting later,
  "Surely we are being punished because of our brother" (Genesis 42:21).
- ***Delayed blessing:*** God's plan to save the family through Joseph still came to pass, but only after years of separation and suffering.

This story has crucial lessons to teach us. Sadly, hatred, rivalry, and unforgiveness are still destroying families today. Favoritism between children, competition over wealth, or resentment over past hurts have blocked the doors of God's blessings in some families. Others are killing themselves, while squabbles have frayed some, and they are languishing in poverty because of disunity.

The Bible warns,
"Anyone who hates a brother or sister is a murderer" (1 John 3:15).

How is your family now? Are you competing with each other and tearing yourselves apart like Jacob's children? If yes, what are you as a Christian doing to remedy the situation?

Joseph's Story – *Family restoration through the power of love*
Love is God's ultimate power for restoring broken lives and families. There is no way you can rebuild a broken family without employing *agape* love. Your family will remain in ruins until one of you rises like Joseph to activate divine love for restoration.

Joseph's life story powerfully illustrates how love can rescue and transform a family torn apart by envy, jealousy, hatred, and rivalry. Such struggles are common in polygamous families, especially across Africa today. We receive counselees who are battling such issues in our office regularly.

As Jacob's favored son, born into a large family with multiple wives, Joseph's position stirred deep resentment among his brothers. Their jealousy grew so fierce that they plotted to kill him, viewing him as a threat to their inheritance and status. Yet God's plan for Joseph was greater than their hatred.

Instead of death, Joseph was sold into slavery and taken to Egypt, where he faced hardship and injustice for about thirteen years. Despite these trials, Joseph remained faithful and refused to let bitterness, regrets, or self-pity consume him. Romans 12:19 reminds us:

> *"Beloved, never avenge yourselves, but leave it to the wrath of God, for it is written, 'Vengeance is mine, I will repay, says the Lord.'"*

That is precisely how Joseph handled the situation, entrusting justice into God's hands.

God's favor elevated him to become the Prime Minister of Egypt (Genesis 41:41-43), giving him the authority to save many from famine. When his brothers came seeking food, Joseph had the chance to repay their betrayal. But moved by love, he forgave them fully and cared for their needs. He said in Genesis 50:20,

> *"As for you, you meant evil against me, but God meant it for good, to bring it about that many people should be kept alive."*

Through love and forgiveness, Joseph restored his family and rescued them from destruction.

Joseph's heart-touching story teaches us that if we are willing, we can triumph over the envy, rivalry, and hatred that are tormenting our families through the power of God's love.

A Matter of Your Heart

One day, God spoke to me in a way that forever changed my perspective. He said, *"The door through which I visit you is your heart."* Then He added, *"My center of operations in your life is your heart. What happens in your life is determined by what is going on in your heart."* From that moment, I realized that the condition of my heart is the decisive factor in whether I experience breakthroughs and the blessings God desires for me.

The matter of your heart is very crucial as it concerns you becoming an agent of restoration in your family. The state of your heart influences every area of your life – your spiritual walk, your marriage, your finances, and your relationships. Without love, your heart becomes closed off to both God and others.

Scripture teaches us this truth: Your heart needs love to grow or prosper. Proverbs 11:25 says, *"A generous person will prosper; whoever refreshes others will be refreshed,"* and Matthew 5:7 reminds us, *"Blessed are the merciful, for they will be shown mercy."* Love is the water of life that produces increase in every area.

Check Your Heart!

Many people face difficulties not because of external forces but because their hearts are in the wrong condition. The Bible identifies five types of evil hearts that can hinder God's work in one's life:

1) *A hardened heart* that resists God's voice and refuses to yield (Exodus 4:21).
2) *A rebellious heart* that refuses submission and authority, leading to strife (Jeremiah 5:23-24).
3) *A proud heart* that is arrogant, unteachable, and looks down on others (Psalm 101:5).
4) *An unbelieving heart* that is skeptical and leads to backsliding (Hebrews 3:12).
5) *A wicked heart* full of hatred, unforgiveness, and revenge (Matthew 6:14-15).

Though your heart is about the size of your clenched fist, it holds incredible power over your life. Proverbs 4:23 commands,

"Guard your heart above all else, for it determines the course of your life."

You cannot experience God's fullness without a heart aligned with His. The Holy Spirit is ready to reveal God's love to your family through your heart. Are you ready? Romans 5:5 says, *"...God has poured out His love into our hearts by the Holy Spirit."* Every believer has received God's love, but this love cannot flow when your heart is not fully surrendered to God. You must be willing to express His love the way He wants, not your way.

If you have discovered that your heart is not right, bring it to God now. He will help you.

Let God Heal Your Heart

Some of the deepest wounds in life are inflicted within the family, through betrayal, favoritism, rejection, abuse, abandonment, or constant conflict. Joseph experienced all of this. His brothers plotted to kill him, sold him into slavery, and covered it up for years. Yet, in the end, he did not become bitter. He chose healing. He understood that God's purpose was greater than his pain.

When his brothers came to Egypt in fear, expecting revenge, Joseph spoke words of grace and perspective:

> *"You intended to harm me, but God intended it all for good" (Genesis 50:20).*

Healing from family wounds doesn't mean denying the pain; it means surrendering it to God. It means choosing forgiveness so that bitterness won't poison your future. Psalm 147:3 reminds us that God heals the brokenhearted and binds up their wounds. What broke you in your family can be the very place God begins to build you. Let healing flow. Let restoration begin, in Jesus' name.

How To Develop a Culture of Love in Your Family

No matter how broken your family is, you can initiate healing and restoration by applying God's principles. Let me show you secrets that can help you restore love in your family.

1. Become a Person of Love

Change always starts with one person. Be that person in your family. Like Joseph, decide to become a person of love – a giver of love. Commit yourself so fully to loving that you stop worrying about whether others will repay you. Follow Christ's example. Romans 5:8 says,

> *"God shows his love for us in that while we were still sinners, Christ died for us."*

Jesus didn't wait for us to change before loving us; He loved us in our sin, and His love changed us.

If you begin loving your family members as they are, they will start to change. Just as wild animals can be tamed through love, difficult family members can be won over by it.

How do you become a person of love? It starts with a sincere prayer to God, asking Him to fill your heart with His love so you can show it to others. He promises to fill you with the Spirit of love (Romans 5:5). We love best when we love in the Spirit.

For example, I began praying daily for God to fill my heart with love. After some months, I noticed a change. I was able to love my family members more freely and genuinely. It has not changed.

2. Sacrifice for Each Other

In family life, sacrificial love means putting the needs of others before our own. For example, the mother works late so her children can study. The father forgoes his dreams to provide stability for his family. Siblings choose peace over winning an argument.

Without sacrifice, love remains just an emotion; with sacrifice, it becomes a force that changes destinies. Jesus taught in John 12:24 that

> **"Unless a grain of wheat falls into the ground and dies, it remains alone; but if it dies, it produces much grain."**

No lasting fruit in a family can come without someone being willing to "Die" to self.

Paul said,

> **"For the love of Christ compels us" (2 Corinthians 5:14).**

True love will push you to do unimaginable things for your family because love makes you brave, patient, and generous. When families practice sacrificial love, they create an atmosphere where God's blessings can freely flow. Let nothing be too big for you to lay down for the sake of your family. Love that costs you nothing is worth nothing; love that costs you everything is worth everything.

3. Practice Giving

Giving is one of the clearest indicators of love. God loved, so He gave. He didn't give leftovers or what cost Him nothing; He gave His very best – He gave Jesus Christ. The Greek word for love in John 3:16, *'agape,'* naturally expresses itself through generosity.

In Acts 20:35, Paul reminds us of Jesus' words:

> **It is more blessed to give than to receive."**

This doesn't mean that receiving is wrong, but that giving brings a deeper, lasting joy because it reflects God's nature.

If you embrace giving, you will create an atmosphere of abundance around your family. Giving isn't just about money; it's also about time, attention, encouragement, and forgiveness. A father who gives time to his children is sowing seeds into their emotional and spiritual well-being. A mother who gives grace to her spouse in moments of weakness is building a safe home.

Stinginess, on the other hand, dries up relationships. Proverbs 11:24-25 says,

> **"There is one who scatters, yet increases more; and there is one who withholds more than is right, but it leads to poverty."**

Love gives freely, trusting God to replenish. A family that obeys God never lacks provision.

Be willing to contribute to family projects. Invest in seeing that your siblings and relatives are established. Don't forget those who helped you when you had nothing.

4. Forgive One Another

Ephesians 4:32 says,

> **"And be kind to one another, tenderhearted, forgiving one another, just as God in Christ forgave you."**

Forgiveness is love's healing balm. It restores relationships, frees hearts, and shuts the door to bitterness. Without forgiveness, your family will remain in cycles of conflict, resentment, and emotional distance.

In Matthew 6:14-15, Jesus warns that if we don't forgive others, God will not forgive us. This is not to punish us, but to remind us that love cannot thrive in a heart that clings to offense.

The Greek word for forgive, *'aphiemi,'* means "To release, let go, or send away." Forgiving your brother or sister is not denying the pain, but releasing them from the debt they owe you.

In a family, forgiveness means letting go of yesterday's arguments, refusing to rehearse past mistakes, and choosing to rebuild trust. It's not always easy, but it is always worth it.

When forgiveness flows, healing follows. Psalm 133 says that unity attracts God's blessing. Forgiveness is the bridge to restoration and unity. Has a family member hurt you? Forgive them! Is there a family member you need forgiveness from? Ask for forgiveness today!

5. Raise Peace Makers

Matthew 5:9 says,

> *"Blessed are the peacemakers, for they will be called children of God."*

The world is divided politically, racially, and socially. But Jesus calls us His followers to be peacemakers, not merely peacekeepers. Peacekeepers avoid conflict; peacemakers confront it with grace and truth, bringing reconciliation.

Romans 12:18 tells us to live at peace with everyone, as much as it depends on us. This kind of peace is not weakness; it's strength under control, guided by God's wisdom (James 3:17).

A family that raises peacemakers becomes a greenhouse for healing in the community and the nations. When children learn to resolve conflict biblically, forgive quickly, and choose unity over pride, they carry those values into every relationship in society. Most of the violence out there is caused by people raised in dysfunctional families.

Peacemakers do not just avoid problems; they actively sow seeds of understanding, mercy, and love. And God Himself promises to call them His children (Matthew 5:9). Peacemakers are not born; they are raised in the house of love.

Don't neglect family conflicts. Take time to resolve them in love, truth, and justice. Go after those who are hurt and don't rest until they return to the sheepfold. Be a peacemaker!

Choose to Love

Love is the foundation you need to build a strong and blessed family. Without it, bitterness, jealousy, and conflict destroy relationships and block God's blessings from your family.

Today, many families are suffering from unresolved disputes and blaming satanic forces, but the real issue is a lack of love. God's love heals, restores, and unites. I want you to seek it passionately. If you become committed to showing compassion to one another, your families will flourish.

We have seen through the stories of Nicky Cruz and Nick Vujicic that love has the power to transform broken lives and establish them in God's purpose. Choose love intentionally, forgive freely, and build a family rooted in God's unending love. You will enjoy His blessings.

PRAYER POINTS
Thanksgiving:

1. *Father, thank You for pouring Your love into our hearts by the Holy Spirit, in Jesus' name.*
2. *Thank You, Lord, for the gift of family and the bond of love that unites us, in Jesus' name.*
3. *Father, I thank You for every testimony of restoration in families through the power of love, in Jesus' name.*
4. *Thank You for demonstrating unconditional love to us through Christ, in Jesus' name.*

Repentance and Renewal:

5. *Father, forgive us for every bitterness, hatred, or unforgiveness that has divided our family, in Jesus' name.*
6. *Lord, forgive us for favoritism, envy, and rivalry that have opened doors to strife, in Jesus' name.*
7. *Father, have mercy on us for failing to walk in sacrificial love towards one another, in Jesus' name.*
8. *Lord, cleanse our hearts from pride, rebellion, and unbelief that hinder Your love, in Jesus' name.*

Forgiveness and Healing:

9. *Lord, heal every wound of rejection, betrayal, and favoritism in our family, in Jesus' name.*
10. *Father, give us tender hearts to forgive one another freely, in Jesus' name.*
11. *Lord, remove every root of bitterness poisoning our relationships, in Jesus' name.*
12. *Father, restore peace and unity where strife and hatred have reigned, in Jesus' name.*
13. *Lord, turn our pain into testimonies of love and restoration, in Jesus' name.*
14. *Father, let forgiveness flow like a river in our family, bringing healing and joy, in Jesus' name.*

Victory Over the Spirit of Hatred, Envy, and Jealousy:

15. *Father, deliver my family from every spirit of hatred and strife seeking to divide us, in Jesus' name.*

16. *Lord, uproot envy and jealousy from our hearts and replace them with contentment, in Jesus' name.*

17. *Father, silence every voice of comparison that fuels envy and resentment in our family, in Jesus' name.*

18. *Lord, destroy every satanic scheme designed to sow hatred among siblings and relatives, in Jesus' name.*

19. *Father, release upon us the spirit of love that rejoices in the success of others, in Jesus' name.*

Victory Over the Spirit of Competition, Division, and Vengeance:

20. *Lord, break the spirit of unhealthy competition and rivalry in my family, in Jesus' name.*

21. *Father, destroy every seed of division and make us one in heart and purpose, in Jesus' name.*

22. *Lord, deliver us from the desire for vengeance and give us hearts of forgiveness, in Jesus' name.*

23. *Father, silence every spirit that thrives on quarrels, revenge, and malice in our family, in Jesus' name.*

24. *Lord, plant in us the spirit of humility, cooperation, and mutual support, in Jesus' name.*

A New Heart and the Baptism of Love:

25. *Father, give every member of my family a new heart that delights in Your love, in Jesus' name.*

26. *Lord, baptize us with the spirit of love that covers multitudes of sins, in Jesus' name.*

27. *Father, remove stony hearts from us and replace them with hearts of flesh, in Jesus' name.*

28. *Lord, let the fire of the Holy Spirit fill our hearts with compassion, mercy, and kindness, in Jesus' name.*

29. *Father, pour out Your perfect love in our family so that fear, hatred, and bitterness will have no place, in Jesus' name.*

Sacrificial and Unconditional Love:

30. *Father, fill our hearts with agape love that bears, believes, hopes, and endures all things, in Jesus' name.*

31. *Lord, help us to put the needs of others in our family above our own, in Jesus' name.*

32. *Father, let sacrificial love be the foundation of every relationship in our household, in Jesus' name.*

33. *Lord, give us grace to love one another unconditionally, regardless of faults and weaknesses, in Jesus' name.*

34. *Father, let our family be rooted and grounded in love, in Jesus' name.*

35. *Lord, let love compel us to forgive, give, and serve one another daily, in Jesus' name.*

Love as a Witness:

36. *Father, let our love for one another be a witness of Christ to the world, in Jesus' name.*

37. *Lord, make our family a channel of love and compassion to others, in Jesus' name.*

38. *Father, let our acts of kindness and generosity draw souls into Your kingdom, in Jesus' name.*

39. *Lord, let love in our home inspire peace and restoration in other families, in Jesus' name.*

40. *Father, may our love overflow to touch our community and generations to come, in Jesus' name.*

Declaration of Divine Judgment:

41. *Let the Lord return the wickedness of the wicked upon their own heads, in Jesus' name.*

42. *Every evil speaker and slanderer against my life — be cut off by the justice of God, in Jesus' name.*

43. *Let the righteous rise up and possess their inheritance without delay, in Jesus' name.*

44. *Every system, policy, or government framed to crush the righteous — be overthrown by heaven's authority, in Jesus' name.*

45. *The Lord my God is my defender; He shall wipe out all wickedness launched against me, in Jesus' name.*

Prophetic Declarations:

46. *We declare that our family shall be built and sustained by love, in Jesus' name.*

47. *We decree that hatred, bitterness, and envy shall not take root in our lineage, in Jesus' name.*

48. *Our family shall flourish in unity, compassion, and forgiveness, in Jesus' name.*

49. *We prophesy that the foundation of love in our family will activate blessings for generations, in Jesus' name.*

50. *Our family shall serve the Lord and be a light to our community and nations, in Jesus' name.*

Chapter 9
Days 25-27

Parental Blessing

"The Lord bless you and keep you; the Lord make his face shine on you and be gracious to you; the Lord turn his face toward you and give you peace" (Numbers 6:24-26).

The anointed words we speak over our children, together with the laying on of hands, act as a powerful channel for transferring God's blessing into their lives. This blessing is not merely symbolic; it carries divine favor, authority, and supernatural power that shape their destiny in meaningful and lasting ways. When a parent speaks God's blessing over their child in faith, it activates spiritual forces that open doors of opportunity, protection, and success.

The Bible teaches that true prosperity and success come from God's blessing. Deuteronomy 8:18 declares,

"But remember the Lord your God, for it is he who gives you the ability to produce wealth."

This verse reminds us that the power to create wealth is a gift from God, emphasizing that any achievement or prosperity we experience is rooted in His blessing. Without God's favor, our efforts alone cannot guarantee lasting success. Proverbs 10:22 further supports this truth:

"The blessing of the Lord brings wealth, without painful toil for it."

This passage highlights a unique characteristic of God's blessing; it enriches without causing sorrow or hardship. Unlike worldly wealth that often comes with stress and struggle, God's blessing brings abundance accompanied by peace and joy.

As parents, it is our spiritual responsibility and privilege to impart this divine blessing to our children. Through prayer, declaration, and the laying on of hands, we invoke God's favor and supernatural empowerment over their lives. This spiritual impartation equips them to overcome obstacles, walk in purpose, and enjoy the fullness of God's provision. In doing so, we establish a foundation for their future success and well-being that goes far beyond material wealth.

We must cultivate a consistent habit of blessing our children. For my father, blessing me has become second nature. Every time I call him, he never ends the conversation without saying, "God bless you and make things easy for you." Those simple prayers from him uplift me both spiritually and emotionally. That's why I always encourage parents to bless their children regularly.

Once, I challenged members of our church to lay hands on their children and bless them every day for a week. By the third week, we received numerous testimonies: students reported breakthroughs in school, and some experienced healing. Even if your children live far away, you can call them each month to speak blessings over their lives.

Remember, your words hold incredible power. Your tongue can deliver, heal, and restore your children. Start using it intentionally and correctly, speaking life and favor into their futures.

A Basket of Fire on My Head

Supernatural impartation happens when your biological parent lays hands on you and blesses you. I am living proof of this. In June 2007, my father visited me in Bamenda. During his stay, my wife and children traveled out of town for two days, leaving us alone at home. One evening, I served him a meal he thoroughly enjoyed. Afterward, I brought him a gift —a traditional Nigerian outfit, one of the most expensive I had purchased at that time.

When he received it, his joy was overwhelming. He asked me to kneel so he could pray for me. I want to emphasize that I did not give the gift seeking a blessing; I simply wanted to honor him. As he laid his hands on my head and prayed from his heart, I felt a powerful anointing pour down over me. Though I don't remember his exact words, the impartation was heavy, and the blessing tangible.

When I stood up, I felt a heavy weight on my head, as if I were carrying a basket of fire. That sensation lasted for two weeks, so real and powerful. Through it, I finally understood what Jacob experienced when Isaac blessed him.

Friend, there is a genuine impartation through parental blessing. This wasn't the first time my father prayed over me, but it was the most profound. Since that day, my life has never been the same. When your parents bless you, a divine blessing comes upon you. Cherish and seek parental blessing.

The Story of Joyce Meyer – *From brokenness to blessing*

Joyce Meyer is one of the authors whose books have had an enormous impact. Her story is a strong message to those who were raised in abusive homes.

She is today a renowned minister, author, and speaker whose influence spans the globe. But behind her success lies a childhood marked by pain and abuse. Instead of receiving a father's love and blessing, Joyce endured physical and emotional abuse from her father. He was often harsh, critical, and unkind, creating an environment of fear and rejection rather than security and affection. This lack of parental blessing left deep emotional scars and caused years of struggle with self-worth and identity.

During one of her ministrations, she said this about her father:

"My father abused me sexually, verbally, mentally, and emotionally, as far back as I can remember, until I was 18. He raped me at least once a week until I was 18. I did a little bit of Maths – my father, who was supposed to keep me safe, raped me a minimum of 200 times before I turned 18."

Despite this, Joyce's story is one of remarkable resilience. She turned to Jesus Christ in faith to heal her broken heart and mind. Through persistent prayer, counseling, and a deep commitment to God's Word, she gradually overcame the trauma and rejection she experienced. Joyce refused to let her father's abuse define her future or dictate her identity. Instead, she chose to embrace God's love, allowing it to transform her pain into purpose. Her experiences equipped her with compassion and insight, which now empower her ministry as she helps millions worldwide overcome similar struggles.

Joyce's life is a testament to the power of God's grace to redeem even the darkest of pasts. Her story reminds us today that while parental blessing is powerful and vital, God's healing can restore those who were denied it. If you have suffered rejection, abuse, or lack of support from your parents, know that your past does not have to limit your future. Like Joyce Meyer, you can rise above your circumstances and become a powerful testimony of God's transforming grace.

What is Parental Blessing?

To understand "Parental Blessing," it is vital to define "Blessing" in a biblical context clearly. The Hebrew word most commonly translated as "Blessing" is *'Barak,'* which means to "Kneel, bless, or praise." The blessing is divine favor, abundance, prosperity, and well-being. Blessing in the Bible is more than good wishes; it is a spiritual impartation of God's power, protection, provision, and approval on someone.

The Greek word for blessing, *'Eulogia,'* means "A spoken expression of good wishes or praise." But again, it points to God's favor bestowed upon a person.

"Parental blessing," therefore, is not just words of kindness or encouragement from parents; it is a spiritual act of transferring God's favor and destiny to their children. It is a foundational seed that helps establish the child's identity, purpose, and protection in life.[9]

The Patriarchs Blessed Their Children

It is common to see in the Bible how the patriarchs blessed their children. In fact, they carried a special blessing, and it was their responsibility to pass it on to their children before their death. How many parents today think of blessing their children before their demise? Maybe some parents fear that if they bless the children, death would snatch them away immediately. So, they finally die without transferring a blessing to their children. After passing on the blessing to Jacob, Isaac still lived some years before dying.

- Abraham blessed Isaac (Genesis 26:3-4). It is not recorded directly, but in Genesis 27, we see Isaac passing it on to his son.
- Isaac blessed Jacob twice (Genesis 27:27-29; 28:1-5).
- Jacob blessed Joseph's son, Manasseh, and Ephraim (Genesis 48:14-16).
- Jacob blessed his children to be established before his death (Genesis 49).
- Moses blessed the tribes of Israel to prosper before his demise (Deuteronomy 33).
- David blessed Solomon to succeed him (1 Chronicles 29:22).
- Job blessed his children after their feasts (Job 1:4-5).
- Jesus welcomed and blessed little children (Mark 10:13-16).

These blessings were spoken with authority and faith and carried supernatural power to influence lives and generations.

What Parental Blessing Will Do in Your Life
Parental blessing is more than words; it is a divine impartation that aligns your children with God's presence, ensuring they thrive under His care. When parents or spiritual leaders pronounce this blessing, they invoke God's power to sustain, favor, and bring wholeness to the blessed.

Numbers 6:22-27 summarizes what parental blessing will do in your life.

> *"The Lord bless you and keep you; the Lord make his face shine on you and be gracious to you; the Lord turn his face toward you and give you peace" (NIV).*

1) **The Blessing Invokes God's Protection –** *"The Lord bless you and keep you"*

The blessing starts with a prayer for God's favor and protection. "Keep you" implies guarding you from harm, both physical and spiritual, and establishing security in your daily life. Bless your children so that they can enjoy security.

2) The Blessing Calls for God's Favor and Grace – "*make his face shine on you and be gracious to you*"

God's "Face shining" is a metaphor for His approval and pleasure. It signifies God's presence, favor, and grace, which open doors, bring success, and enable the blessed to experience His kindness. Bless your children to enjoy favor and open doors.

3) The Blessing Brings Peace – "*turn his face toward you and give you peace*"

The final part speaks of shalom, a Hebrew word meaning peace, completeness, and well-being. This blessing encompasses peace in every aspect of life: spiritual, emotional, relational, and physical. Bless your children so that they can enjoy peace and emotional stability.

Why curse your child when your blessing can make them great?

Negative Pronouncements Cancelled

In the realm of parental blessings, the power of a name carries profound spiritual weight. Pronouncements made by parents, especially through the names they give their children, can either unlock destiny or trap it.

A striking example is Rachel's naming of her son Benjamin. Before her death, Rachel called him *Ben-Oni*, meaning **"Son of my sorrow"** (Genesis 35:18). This name was a curse, reflecting grief rather than blessing. Jacob, his father, immediately changed the name to *Benjamin*, meaning **"Son of the right hand."** A name signifying strength, favor, and a place of honor. Jacob understood the principle of parental blessing and reversed the negative pronouncement by renaming and blessing his son.

Similarly, the mother of Jabez gave him a name meaning **"Sorrow"** or **"He makes sorrowful"** (1 Chronicles 4:9). Unlike Benjamin, Jabez's father is not mentioned, and there was no paternal blessing to counteract the negative impact of his name. Consequently, Jabez suffered under the weight of that bad name until he boldly went before God, prayed for deliverance, and God granted his request (1 Chronicles 4:10). His story teaches us that in the absence of parental reversal, one can seek God's intervention to break free from negative pronouncements.

Another tragic case is **Ichabod**, whose name means *"No glory"* (1 Samuel 4:21-22). His mother gave him this name after hearing of the loss of the Ark and her husband. After Ichabod's birth, the glory departed from Israel, and the Bible never mentions him again. His story illustrates how a negative name can symbolize the loss of destiny and divine favor.

Are you trapped by a negative name or pronouncements spoken over you? Jesus paid the ultimate price on the cross for your freedom. Before His death, He declared, *"It is finished" (John 19:30)*, signaling that every curse and bondage has been broken. As a child of God, your past no longer defines you; it has been washed clean by the blood of Jesus Christ. Claim your freedom and blessings today. The power of every negative name is broken in Jesus' name. You will prosper and walk in favor, just like Benjamin and Jabez.

Activating Parental Blessings

Three things about you can touch your parents' hearts and release powerful blessings or curses into your life:

1. Costly Acts of Love

Acts of love that require effort and sacrifice from you will move your parents to bless you. Isaac said to Esau,

> **"Prepare me delicious food that I love, and bring it to me so I may eat it and bless you before I die" (Genesis 27:4).**

Esau's gift was meant to stir Isaac's heart and release the Abrahamic blessing on him. I told you how my gift to my dad touched his heart, and he blessed me.

You must be intentional to provoke your parents' blessings. Care for them when they are ill, meet their urgent needs, do what they love, or spend time serving them. Many assume honoring God's servants in church is enough. They invest a lot in taking care of their spiritual leaders in church, neglecting their parents. Is it because you think your parents are not anointed? Never forget this: your biological parents, whether born again or not, hold spiritual authority over you as well. If you honor them, God will bless you.

The Bible says:

> *"Honor your father and mother" (this is the first commandment with a promise), "that it may go well with you and that you may live long in the land" (Ephesians 6:2-3).*

Note, it didn't say, "Honor your apostle, prophet, or pastor." It says, "Honor your father and mother." Your spiritual parents, as well as your biological parents, all have their place. Treat them as the Bible has instructed.

Honoring your biological parents will unlock prosperity and longevity in your life.

Even if your parents are abusive or involved in troubling behaviors, this does not permit you to disrespect them. Do your part by honoring them, and trust God to handle the rest.

2. Deep Provocation

Disrespecting or provoking your parents can bring a curse into your life. This is what the Bible says about it.

> *"If someone curses their father or mother, their lamp will be snuffed out in pitch darkness" (Proverbs 20:20).*
>
> *"Cursed is anyone who dishonors their father or mother" (Deuteronomy 27:16 NIV).*

Reuben, Jacob's eldest son, dishonored his father by sleeping with Jacob's concubine, Bilhah (Genesis 35:22). This was a serious breach of family trust and a direct challenge to his father's authority. On his deathbed, Jacob declared,

> *"Unstable as water, you shall not excel, because you went up to your father's bed; then you defiled it" (Genesis 49:4).*

Reuben's sin cost him his birthright and leadership, and his tribe lost prominence. This shows that disrespect toward parents leads to a lasting loss of honor, blessing, and status.

Many are struggling in life because they have knowingly or unknowingly provoked curses on themselves through parental disrespect. If you have unresolved issues with your parents, humble yourself and seek reconciliation. I once preached a message titled "Parental Blessing." A brother in our church, facing repeated setbacks in business, decided to return home. He brought gifts for his parents, waited patiently for two days, and then asked for forgiveness and a blessing. Though his father was once angry that he chose business over education, that day, his father blessed him with tears. From then on, his fortunes changed, and he never faced such struggles again. You can experience the same transformation by doing what Brother Paul's example.

3. When Your child is hurt by someone

The heart of a true parent is deeply moved when their child is hurt. When this happens, it can unleash powerful prayers that disrupt the kingdom of darkness and bring freedom to your child. Jairus, a synagogue leader, exemplified this when he urgently pleaded with Jesus to heal his dying daughter (Mark 5:22-24). His desperate fight to save her life led Jesus to raise her from the dead, showing the strength of faith and a parent's plea for deliverance.

However, such a provoked heart can also lead a parent into sin if objectivity is lost. Many parents I pray with insist their child has done nothing wrong, especially in cases of marital conflict. They often blindly support their child and accuse their child's spouse of being the root of the problem. This is dangerous. That is why it is not wise to report your marital differences to your parents quickly.

Dear parent, do this when your child's struggles stir your heart: start by thanking God for what He has already done in their marriage. Then, intercede for forgiveness for both your child and their spouse. Pray earnestly for their hearts to soften and for God's intervention to heal the situation. Engage in spiritual warfare, but always ask God to fill your heart and theirs with wisdom and love.

If you want God's help, you must handle the problem according to His plan for marriage as revealed in the Bible. Humble yourself through fasting and prayer to discern God's perspective and guidance on how to address the situation rightly.

14 Moments To Communicate Parental Blessings

As a parent, you have the spiritual authority to release God's favor, protection, and empowerment in their lives. I want to show you strategic times when you, as a godly parent, should impart blessings to your children. Intentional parental blessings during these strategic moments affirm your child's identity, purpose, and destiny.

1) ***Dedication at Birth:*** Hannah dedicated Samuel to the Lord (1 Samuel 1:27-28). While you organize a dedication ceremony for your baby in church, set aside a time to bless and speak prophetically to the destiny of your child. Do it with your spouse if you are believers.

2) ***During Birthdays:*** Jacob blessed his sons (Genesis 49). While the Bible doesn't explicitly mention birthday blessings, it is a time for parental impartation.

3) ***Before Marriage:*** Rebecca's parents blessed her before she left home for marriage (Genesis 24:60). Isaac blessed Jacob before marriage and family life (Genesis 27; 28:1-10). Bless your children before they leave your home for marriage. This is different from the blessing in church. Ask for God's favor and blessings on their union.

4) ***Before the Start of the School Year:*** Solomon prayed for wisdom before leading Israel (1 Kings 3:9). Parents can pray blessings for wisdom and success before their children begin studies.

5) ***Before Traveling:*** Abraham blessed his servant before sending him to find a wife for Isaac (Genesis 24:1-9). Bless your children before they travel. Ask for God's protection and guidance. My father always prays for me before I travel out of Cameroon. Sometimes he calls me when I'm sitting on the plane, about to take off.

6) **When Sick:** Jesus healed and blessed the sick (Mark 1:40-42). Pray and lay hands on your children for healing and restoration when they are ill.
You can anoint them. My wife and I have seen several divine interventions in the lives of our kids when they were sick.

7) **When Facing Crisis:** God has promised to give your children peace and divine establishment. Pray for them when they are hurting or facing tough times (Isaiah 54:13-17). Go to them or call them to come to you for ministration. You can also minister to them virtually.

8) **Starting a New Job:** Bless children entering new work environments to receive favor and success (Numbers 6:22-27). If you live in the same town, go to your child's office and pray.

9) **Moving to a New House:** Bless your child's new home for peace and prosperity (Psalm 91). Some houses are infested with demons and need to be sanitized spiritually. Join your children to do it if you are around them.

10) **Starting to Build (House, Business, etc.):** Solomon's temple construction began with prayer and blessing (1 Kings 8). Bless the project your child is starting. I called my parents to join my wife and me, and a pastor I had invited, to bless our house project before we started the construction.

11) **Dedicating a New House:** Solomon dedicated the temple with a prayer and blessing (2 Chronicles 6). Join your children to bless their new houses, to invite God's presence and protection.

12) **When Planning to Give Birth:** Bless your children's spouses or family during pregnancy and childbirth. Please

give them the necessary assistance during this period. One woman of God testified that if she had not been present at the hospital during the first delivery experience of her daughter, she would have lost her. Mothers, be there for them!

*13) **Before Writing Exams:*** Daniel sought God's wisdom and favor (Daniel 1:17). Bless them before they go in for their exams. Pray for clarity, memory, and success in exams.

*14) **Before Important Interviews:*** Esther approached the king with favor (Esther 5:1-2). Bless your child for favor, confidence, and success in interviews.

Parental blessings can be imparted at the family altar or remotely through online connections. Parents can lay hands, anoint with oil, or speak blessing prayers over their children.

Bless Your Children

Parental blessing is a divine impartation of God's favor, authority, and protection over children, profoundly shaping their destiny. It is rooted in Scripture, as seen in Numbers 6:24-26, Deuteronomy 8:18, and Proverbs 10:22. The blessing will open doors to success, peace, and prosperity for your children. We have seen how biblical patriarchs, such as Abraham, Isaac, Jacob, and Moses, modeled this practice by blessing their children and tribes.

I encourage you to bless your children consistently, through prayer, declaration, and laying on of hands. This will activate God's favor on them. I do it for my children weekly. If you have no parents to bless you, seek God's grace for restoration like Joyce Meyer.

Apply this message in your family and see the mighty breakthroughs that will begin to happen.

PRAYER POINTS

Thanksgiving:

1. Father, thank You for the gift of parental blessing that shapes destinies, in Jesus' name.
2. Lord, I thank You for the blessings and prayers spoken by my parents and spiritual leaders, in Jesus' name.
3. Father, I thank You for the promise that Your blessing makes rich and adds no sorrow, in Jesus' name.
4. Thank You for the generational blessings available to us in Christ Jesus, in Jesus' name.

Repentance and Mercy:

5. Father, forgive me and my family for dishonoring our parents through words, attitudes, or actions, in Jesus' name.
6. Lord, forgive us for every negative pronouncement we have made over our children, in Jesus' name.
7. Father, forgive our parents for words of anger, rejection, or curses spoken over us, in Jesus' name.
8. Lord, have mercy on us for neglecting to consistently bless our children with words of life, in Jesus' name.

Activating Parental Blessings:

9. Lord, help me to use my words to impart blessings and not curses over my children, in Jesus' name.
10. Father, release Your anointing upon my lips so that my declarations will shape godly destinies, in Jesus' name.
11. Lord, let every blessing spoken by our parents align our families with Your purpose, in Jesus' name.
12. Father, let parental blessings unlock favor and open doors of opportunity for our children, in Jesus' name.
13. Lord, bless our children with wisdom, knowledge, and understanding for success, in Jesus' name.
14. Father, may our parental blessings serve as a shield of protection over our children, in Jesus' name.

Breaking Negative Pronouncements:

15. Every negative pronouncement spoken over my life, be cancelled by the blood of Jesus, in Jesus' name.

16. *Lord, reverse every curse of sorrow, limitation, and rejection placed upon any member of my family, in Jesus' name.*
17. *Father, silence the power of every evil name working against my destiny, in Jesus' name.*
18. *Lord, heal every wound and scar caused by parental rejection, in Jesus' name.*
19. *Father, release Your blessing to replace every negative decree over my household, in Jesus' name.*

Honoring Parents:

20. *Lord, give us wisdom to honor our parents in love and humility, in Jesus' name.*
21. *Father, let our acts of kindness and service to parents provoke generational blessings, in Jesus' name.*
22. *Lord, help us to value and care for our parents in their time of need, in Jesus' name.*
23. *Father, let reconciliation and forgiveness flow between parents and children in our family, in Jesus' name.*
24. *Lord, let honoring parents unlock prosperity and long life for us and our children, in Jesus' name.*

Let Parental Blessing Flow:

25. *Lord, let the blessings of Abraham, Isaac, and Jacob flow through our lineage, in Jesus' name.*
26. *Father, help us to learn from Jacob and bless our children with words of destiny, in Jesus' name.*
27. *Lord, raise fathers and mothers in our family who will speak prophetically like Moses, in Jesus' name.*
28. *Father, let us model Jesus' example of welcoming and blessing our children, in Jesus' name.*
29. *Lord, make us parents who constantly cover our children in prayer like Job, in Jesus' name.*
30. *Father, let our parental blessings bring stability, peace, and generational impact, in Jesus' name.*

Deliverance for Children in Bondage:

31. *Father, deliver our children from every bondage of addiction, immorality, and peer pressure, in Jesus' name.*
32. *Lord, break every yoke of fear, depression, and mental captivity holding our children bound, in Jesus' name.*

33. *Father, release our children from every ancestral curse and generational chain limiting their destiny, in Jesus' name.*

34. *Lord, set our children free from the grip of occultism, witchcraft, and ungodly covenants, in Jesus' name.*

35. *Father, let the blood of Jesus secure total deliverance and victory for our children, in Jesus' name.*

Recovery of Family Blessings:

36. *Father, let every blessing stolen from our family line be recovered sevenfold, in Jesus' name.*

37. *Lord, restore the financial, spiritual, and marital blessings that the enemy has diverted from our household, in Jesus' name.*

38. *Father, let every blessing buried in ancestral covenants be released to our generation, in Jesus' name.*

39. *Lord, recover for us the honor, opportunities, and favor that were lost through disobedience, in Jesus' name.*

40. *Father, let generational blessings flow again in our family, bringing prosperity and divine increase, in Jesus' name.*

Rise of Giants in Your Family:

41. *Father, raise men and women of faith, vision, and influence in our family who will stand as giants in their generation, in Jesus' name.*

42. *Lord, let leaders, kingdom financiers, and innovators emerge from our household to impact nations, in Jesus' name.*

43. *Father, anoint our children to be spiritual giants who will tear down strongholds and establish Your kingdom, in Jesus' name.*

44. *Lord, raise generational trailblazers from our family in education, business, ministry, and governance, in Jesus' name.*

45. *Father, we prophesy that our lineage shall never lack giants of wisdom, excellence, and divine authority, in Jesus' name.*

Revival in Families in the Nation

46. *Father, pour out Your Spirit upon families across this nation and ignite true revival, in Jesus' name.*

47. *Lord, restore family altars of prayer, worship, and the Word in every household, in Jesus' name.*

48. *Father, let every family in this land turn away from idolatry and compromise, and return fully to You, in Jesus' name.*

49. *Lord, raise families as centers of light, holiness, and evangelism that will transform communities, in Jesus' name.*

50. *Father, let revival fire in families spread across the nation until righteousness exalts the land, in Jesus' name.*

Chapter 10
Days 28-30

A Lasting Legacy

"A good man leaves an inheritance to his children's children, but the wealth of the sinner is stored up for the righteous" (Proverbs 13:22).

What do you want to be remembered for when you're no longer here?

Some people live without purpose, giving little thought to the future. They ignore a timeless principle that governs life: the law of seed and harvest. Galatians 6:7 says it plainly:

"Whatever a man sows, that he will also reap."

Do you know that every choice you make today, seen or unseen, is a seed, and every seed produces a harvest?

Think about your family five, ten, or fifty years from now. What future do you envision? Maybe you dream of raising children who grow into honorable leaders or desire a strong, united, God-fearing family. Those dreams are good, but without action, they will perish. Your obedience, sacrifice, and godly investments today shape the future you hope to see.

Scripture gives us both inspiration and warning. Abraham's and David's families were blessed for generations because of their faithfulness. David, especially, received a promise that led to the birth of Christ because he walked in righteousness. In contrast, Saul's family was cut off because of disobedience. One person's life can either lift or destroy an entire lineage.

The way you live today will either prosper or ruin your lineage in the years to come. Let me ask you these pertinent questions: "If you knew your daily choices would impact your children's future, how would you live?" "If you were certain you'd be rewarded in heaven for obedience, or face eternal consequences for rebellion in hell, what changes would you make now?"

Unfortunately, many live with the erroneous mindset, "Let's enjoy today; tomorrow will sort itself out." But that attitude is dangerous. According to Galatians 6:8, you will reap whatever you sow. Every day, you sow seeds through your words, actions, values, and example. The real question is: what kind of legacy are you building? Will your life point your family toward God or away from Him? Will your obedience pave the way for blessing, or will your carelessness leave curses and sorrow?

A lasting legacy isn't accidental. It is born from intentional living, consistent faith, and Christ-centered sacrifice. And the time to start sowing is now!

A Scary Assignment

In September 2023, I spent three intense days at Babcock University, Nigeria, completing a transformational leadership training with the Institute of National Transformation (INT), led by Prof. Vincent Anigbogu.

It was the most demanding program I've ever attended. We had less than one hour of sleep per day, deliberately structured to train us to lead under extreme pressure. We received several challenging tasks, but one assignment stood out; it terrified us. Some students refused to do it at first, but Prof. Vincent warned, "Anyone who can't face this will be eliminated." That left no choice. Everyone submitted.

And here's the assignment:

"Write a realistic obituary that reflects your life as it stands right now; not what you hope people would say, but what they would truthfully say today."

Answer the following:
- (1) **What would be written about you?**
- (2) Focus on your current lifestyle, your character, and how others perceive you.
- (3) **What accomplishments would be mentioned?**
  List any achievements that define your life today – educational, professional, personal, or spiritual.
- (4) **Who would grieve for you?**
  Consider your family, friends, church, or community. Who would feel your loss?
- (5) **Who would attend your funeral, and how many would show up?**
  Think honestly about your level of impact. Would it be a small family gathering, or would a broader community show up?

Compare this version of your life to your God-given calling. What have you done or left undone for the Kingdom of God?"

This is my obituary, which I wrote.

"Godson T. Nembo, aged 49, former Director of Foreign Missions at Full Gospel Mission Cameroon and founder of the Christian Restoration Network (CRN), passed away on September 16, 2023.

He was the author of over 27 books, including the widely read daily devotional prayer guide, *Prayer Storm Daily Prayer Guide*, which has impacted countless lives worldwide. With nearly one million copies of his works in circulation globally, his influence reached far beyond borders.

Godson was known for his tireless efforts in mobilizing national spiritual awakening. He organized the annual 30-day national fasts, prayer camps, and various intercessory programs dedicated to seeing God move in Cameroon and the nations. His passion for family restoration, discipleship, and revival left a lasting mark on many.

He was a father figure to many widows and orphans, generously sponsoring their education and well-being. His family, the people he supported, and the many hurting, oppressed, and demonized individuals he ministered to are grieving deeply at his passing.

His funeral will be attended by a diverse array of mourners, including governors, public administrators, traditional rulers, military officials, commissioners, business leaders, and individuals from all walks of life – a testament to the wide-reaching impact of his life and ministry."

Can You Also Do The Assignment?

You may take time to complete this exercise, as I did, or you may hesitate out of fear. But remember, remember that Paul viewed his death as a moment of triumph and glory, because his deepest desire was to be with Christ. He said,

"For to me to live is Christ, and to die is gain" (Philippians 1:21).

For him, death was not loss; it was fulfillment (2 Timothy 4:7).

Are you afraid of death? It may be a sign that you're not truly free. Anyone who isn't ready for the Kingdom of Heaven will naturally fear the end. But when you've lived a life of purpose, obedience, and surrender to God, you can face death without fear or shame, before God, before others, and before yourself.

One day, you will leave this world. It may happen when you least expect it. I introduced this assignment on the obituary to challenge you to live your life with purpose, with eternity in view. You must leave behind a glorious legacy.

The Long-Term Impact of a Godly or Ungodly Legacy

Throughout this book, we've seen how both godliness and ungodliness can shape the destiny of entire families. By examining various examples from Scripture and history, we've uncovered the profound and lasting impact of a person's choices.

In this chapter, I won't burden you with many stories. My goal is simple: to challenge you to live intentionally, leaving behind a legacy that honors God and blesses future generations. That said, we will briefly reflect on one last powerful historical comparison, the story of Max Jukes and Jonathan Edwards.

A.E. Winship (1845-1933) was a respected American educator, author, and speaker, known for highlighting the role of character, values, and upbringing in shaping future generations. He was the first to document the contrasting legacies of Max Jukes and Jonathan Edwards in his influential work, *"Jukes-Edwards: A Study in Education and Heredity," a comparison that* we will briefly explore in this chapter.

While carrying out research in a New York prison, E. A Winship noticed something unusual. As he examined the records, he found that several inmates came from the same family line. This sparked his curiosity. He wanted to understand how so many people from one family ended up in prison. A man once told me a similar pathetic story that there were four of his brothers in the Yaounde Central Prison. He added that his family was so poor that if any of them had an issue needing 50,000 FCFA (About $95), they wouldn't be able to handle it.

Winship found out that the prisoners who caught his attention in the New York Prison were from the family of a man named Max Jukes. Max was an atheist who lived without regard for God or moral principles. He married a woman of similar character, and together they lived irresponsibly. Over time, their children and grandchildren followed in their footsteps.

Winship traced about 1,200 descendants of Max Jukes, and what he found was shocking:

- 310 became paupers (Destitute and dependent on others),
- 130 were convicted criminals,
- 190 public prostitutes
- 60 were thieves,
- 7 were murderers,
- and 100 were alcoholics.

Not one was known for making a positive contribution to society.

This troubling discovery led Winship to ask another question: "What happens when a person lives a godly life?" To find out, he studied the descendants of Jonathan Edwards, a Christian pastor and theologian from the 1700s. Edwards was a man of deep faith who married a godly woman. Together, they raised their children with discipline, prayer, and a strong sense of purpose.

Winship traced around 1,400 of Edwards' descendants and found very different results:

- 300 became pastors or missionaries,
- 120 became university professors,
- 110 became lawyers,
- 30 became judges,
- 13 were college presidents,
- 3 served in Congress,
- and 1 became Vice President of the United States.

The comparison was clear: one man's godless life led to generations of destruction, while another man's godly life produced generations of influence, leadership, and blessing.

This teaches us that our choices matter, not just for us, but for those who come after us. The legacy you leave begins with how you live today. You can decide to change the future of your family now!

What is Legacy?

The English word "Legacy" comes from the Latin *'legatus,'* meaning an ambassador, envoy, or one who is sent to represent. Over time, it came to mean something handed down, whether a mission, property, or reputation.

In Hebrew, the word often associated with legacy is *'nachalah'*, translated as "Inheritance" or "Possession." It implies something passed from one generation to another – whether it be land, a blessing, or a responsibility.

In Greek (New Testament), the word *'kleronomia'* is used, meaning "Inheritance" or "Heritage." It carries the sense of receiving what rightfully belongs to you through family or covenant.

So biblically, legacy is more than material; it is about what you entrust to or send to the next generation.

7 Types of Legacies

These are godly legacies you can pass on to the next generation.

1) ***Spiritual Legacy*** – Passing down genuine faith in Christ and devotion to God ensures that future generations walk in His ways (Deuteronomy 6:6-7; 2 Timothy 1:5; Psalm 78:4).

2) ***Moral Legacy*** – Living with integrity, justice, and truth leaves a name more valuable than riches (Proverbs 22:1; Micah 6:8; Proverbs 20:7).

3) ***Relational Legacy*** – Modeling love, forgiveness, and unity in the family creates peace that blesses generations (Colossians 3:13-14; Ephesians 4:32; Psalm 133:1).

4) ***Intellectual/Skills Legacy*** – Passing down wisdom, knowledge, and skills equips children to succeed and glorify God (Proverbs 22:6; Ecclesiastes 7:12; Exodus 35:30–31).

5) ***Financial/Material Legacy*** – Providing responsibly for one's family and leaving an inheritance builds stability and honor (Proverbs 13:22; 1 Timothy 5:8; 2 Corinthians 12:14).

6) ***Service Legacy*** – A life of generosity, sacrifice, and service inspires others and outlives the giver (Acts 20:35; Matthew 5:16; Hebrews 6:10).

7) ***Creativity Legacy*** – Using God-given imagination and innovation to bless society leaves behind works, ideas, and solutions that impact future generations (Genesis 1:27; Exodus 35:31; Matthew 5:16).

Your Legacy Is in the Foundation

Every lasting legacy begins with a strong foundation. What you build in life will only be as secure as the base it stands on. Many people are concerned about the beauty and size of their "Building" – their career, ministry, business, or family- but God is more concerned with the foundation.

Psalm 11:3 asks,

"When the foundations are being destroyed, what can the righteous do?"

The answer is clear: without a right foundation, even the righteous cannot preserve what is built. A cracked or corrupt foundation guarantees eventual collapse. A poorly constructed bridge with cracks can only serve for a time. It must crumble. A magnificent skyscraper can rise quickly, but if its foundation is shallow, the first earthquake will bring it down. In contrast, a building with deep, reinforced foundations may take longer to complete, but it will outlast every storm.

What are you building? Will it stand the times? Some people don't care how they make money or advance in life. If you climb to the top by crushing others, or you prosper by cheating others, a day of reckoning will come when your family will pay the debt. This is the truth God wants us to learn. Shortcuts do not take us far; they complicate the journey.

One day, my son shared something that profoundly shocked me. He said, *"Daddy, one of my acquaintances told me, 'If you really knew what you carry, you would already be very wealthy.'"* I understood exactly what the young man was telling my son – he was suggesting that I should use the ministry to pursue money at all costs. I looked at my son and answered plainly: *"I will never manipulate people or compromise my standards for the sake of money or fame."*

Whenever I face temptation, I immediately think about the consequences my actions could have on my children. I ask myself, "What if I give in and bring God's judgment upon them?" I often recall Gehazi, who brought leprosy upon himself and his descendants due to his deceitful actions with Naaman (2 Kings 5).

Why should a moment of selfish pleasure condemn my lineage to years of pain? Many families today struggle under the weight of evil foundations laid by their parents. Instead of breaking these sinful patterns, some believers continue in the same cycles – immorality, alcoholism, dishonesty, and wickedness – yet still expect breakthroughs. It is time to stop that empty religion and become serious with God.

If true change is to come, you must choose to lay a new foundation of righteousness for your family, one that breaks the curse of the past and secures a future of blessing. Sadly, some preachers today twist Scripture to exploit vulnerable souls, robbing them of their hard-earned income. But the truth is, every thief behind the pulpit will face judgment. Consider Eli and his sons in *1 Samuel 2*. They defiled God's altar with greed, and both they and their children suffered horrific consequences. Is that what you want for your family? Mind what you are building now!

How To Build A Legacy That Blesses Generations

Building a legacy that blesses future generations doesn't happen by accident. It requires intention, faith, and consistency. Here are key biblical principles to guide you:

1. Fear God and Transfer Godly Values

The foundation of every lasting legacy is the **fear of the Lord**. Proverbs 9:10 says,

> *"The fear of the Lord is the beginning of wisdom, and knowledge of the Holy One is understanding."*

Every generation leaves something behind. Some pass down blessings, favor, land, money, or honor; others pass down curses, shame, poverty, strife, or witchcraft. But the greatest legacy you can leave to your family or generation is the fear of God and godly values.

According to the verse above, wisdom for life begins with reverence for God. When you, as a parent, build your life on this foundation and intentionally transfer it to your children and those under you, you secure a legacy that outlives you.

The fear of God is crucial because it guides our choices, preserves our heritage, and protects our families from destruction. If you are a man or woman who fears God, you will not cheat in business, oppress the weak, or betray your spouse. Why? Because you fear God and know that if you sow seeds of sin, your family will harvest disaster.

David's lineage enjoyed generational blessings because of his righteous walk with God, while Saul's lineage was cut off because of disobedience and idolatry. Even in Cameroon today, corruption, immorality, greed, witchcraft, and strife are destroying families. But if you choose the fear of God, you will lay new foundations for the prosperity of your children. Jonathan Edwards and his wife lived in fear of God; their legacy speaks volumes.

I want you to know this: legacies can be broken or built. Some families inherit alcoholism, dishonesty, or witchcraft, but you should pass down prayer, integrity, and service to your family. The fear of God and the transfer of godly values remain the surest path to a lasting and blessed legacy. Decide to live and love like Jesus Christ.

2. Establish a Family Vision

Every family needs a clear direction to prosper and flourish. Without vision, families wander and are easily destroyed by the pressures of life. Proverbs 29:18 says,

"Where there is no vision, the people perish."

Your family vision should establish spiritual, moral, and practical goals, and explain why those values are important. Such a vision, when written down, will unite your family and create a purpose that spans across generations.

A Christ-centered family vision must be anchored in God's Word.
"But as for me and my household, we will serve the Lord"
(Joshua 24:15).

Parents must declare and model this commitment so children know where the family stands. A vision might include daily prayer, honesty in business, education for every child, or community service. A man said his vision is that all his children and grandchildren should know Christ personally and serve Him. Secondly, he set the goal to build a house for each of them before they turn twenty-one.

Practically, you can sit together as a family and write out your goals. For example: "We are a family that fears God, works hard, forgives quickly, and helps the needy." Display it at home. Regularly revisit it. This gives children identity and direction.

This family in Bamenda gathered every New Year's Day to pray, reflect on the past year, and set family goals for the new year. Today, their grown children testify that those meetings kept them united and disciplined, even when opportunities for corruption or immorality came their way.

Remember, vision must be lived, not just spoken. Jesus said,
"Seek first the kingdom of God and his righteousness, and
all these things will be added to you" (Matthew 6:33).

If you put God at the center of your family vision, you will leave behind more than wealth. You will leave behind a blessed legacy.

3. Put Your House in Order

Don't leave confusion behind. A godly legacy demands that you organize your home, finances, and relationships with wisdom. Live in a way that reflects order, not chaos, so your children inherit peace and stability rather than battles and shame. 1 Corinthians 14:40 reminds us:

> **"But everything should be done in a fitting and orderly way."**

One practical step is to write a will. Sadly, many in Cameroon resist this, believing that writing a will invites death. That is a deception. Writing a will is not a curse; it is wisdom. It secures your children's future and prevents unnecessary strife. I once heard an uncle say, "I will never write a will." Such thinking leaves families in chaos. In your will, remember all your children and assign responsibility wisely. I've seen men choose daughters to succeed them, even when sons were alive, because they trusted them to protect the family's name. Don't entrust your legacy to someone irresponsible.

I know of a family in Yaoundé who registered several hectares of land in Etoudi in the name of a brother they only met in church. He had no blood connection with them. Today, he signs as the official "Landowner" whenever plots are sold. This happened because that was the only way to put their house in order.

Pay your debts if you can. Don't leave your children embarrassed by creditors. Settle disputes while alive. King David modeled this; before his death, he prepared his household and dedicated his wealth for God's temple (1 Chronicles 29). His successor, Solomon, became the wealthiest man on earth.

Like David, include God in your will. Assign money, a land, or a house to God's work. While writing this chapter, I received a call about someone who wants to offer a piece of land for God's work. He said, "Something must be built for God on my land." Let your sacrifices to God lay a foundation of prosperity for your family.

Without order, your family cannot prosper. A legacy of order is a legacy of blessing.

4. Develop Family Gifts

Every family has God-given talents and callings, and part of leaving a lasting legacy is to discover, nurture, and pass them on. These gifts may be academic, artistic, spiritual, or leadership-related, but they must be cultivated and used for God's glory. Romans 12:6 reminds us:

> *"We have different gifts, according to the grace given to each of us."*

I know of a man who was a gifted craftsman. When he died, none of his children inherited his workshop. It was shut down, and his children scattered, looking for odd jobs. What a loss of legacy! On the other hand, I once watched an American father training his four-year-old son to handle crocodiles. The boy represented the third generation in the family business, and people came from far to visit their crocodile resort. In another case, a Hollywood makeup artist in the 1920s invited his children into his work. Today, after over one hundred years, they have developed rare cosmetic products that now serve the wealthy worldwide. These families built legacies by passing down their trades.

Why is it that in our context, many children do not continue with the trades of their parents? After graduating from university, why not return to your family trade and raise it to another level by applying modern techniques? In biblical times, this was a common practice. Jesus was called a carpenter because Joseph, his earthly father, was a carpenter (Mark 6:3). Trades, skills, and callings were often passed down through families.

As parents, we must identify our children's talents and nurture them. After writing over thirty books, I have written the first book with my daughter, and I believe she will write many in the future. By nurturing her gift, I am sowing into her future.

Your family will never lack if you develop the gifts God has already planted within you.

5. Give God a Place in Family Milestones

Every milestone in the family – birthdays, weddings, funerals, and even the writing of a will should honor God. These are not just social events; they are opportunities to point people to Christ and strengthen family faith and unity. Proverbs 16:3 says,

> *"Commit to the Lord whatever you do, and he will establish your plans."*

Sadly, many Christians spend extravagantly on celebrations but leave God out. This should not be so. Every time you plan a ceremony, include the

Gospel. Budget for Bibles, tracts, or Christian literature. One couple I know ordered hundreds of copies of our devotional *Prayer Storm* and placed one on every seat during their wedding. Guests not only celebrated the marriage but also went home with spiritual food.

Family milestones gather relatives, friends, and entire communities. These moments must connect people to God. Funerals, for example, often attract huge crowds. Why not view them as cost-free opportunities to preach Christ intentionally? I once advised the children of a generous old man who had passed away: "The best way to honor your father is to bless your village." They listened and electrified their community, rather than wasting millions on entertainment. One of my cousins also applied this principle. Instead of organizing a massive death celebration for her grandmother, she built a school in her honor. The school bears Grandma's name. Today, her name lives on because children learn there every day. That is a lasting memorial.

Take advantage of every family milestone to glorify God and strengthen relationships. Let your celebrations not just honor people but draw many to Christ. A family that puts God at the center of its milestones builds a legacy that time cannot erase.

What Do You Want To Be Remembered For?
Legacy is not built in a day; it is the product of daily choices, obedience, and faith in God. Scripture reminds us that whatever we sow today, we will reap tomorrow (Galatians 6:7). The lives of Max Jukes and Jonathan Edwards illustrate how godlessness breeds destruction, while godliness produces blessings across generations. A true legacy is not just about money or property, but also encompasses spiritual, moral, relational, intellectual, financial, service, and creative values passed on to future generations. The question remains: will your life point your family toward God or away from Him? A lasting legacy begins with intentional, Christ-centered living today.

PRAYER POINTS
Thanksgiving:
1. *Father, thank You for the gift of family and the opportunity to leave a godly legacy, in Jesus' name.*

2. *Lord, I thank You for the blessings and examples of righteous men and women who shaped generations, in Jesus' name.*
3. *Thank You for the seeds of faith, obedience, and sacrifice already sown in our family line, in Jesus' name.*
4. *Father, I thank You because Your Word assures us that the righteous leave an inheritance for their children's children, in Jesus' name.*

Repentance and Mercy:

5. *Lord, forgive us for living carelessly without considering the legacy we are leaving behind, in Jesus' name.*
6. *Father, have mercy on us for every ungodly seed of immorality, dishonesty, or corruption sown in our family line, in Jesus' name.*
7. *Lord, forgive us for neglecting to transfer godly values and examples to our children, in Jesus' name.*
8. *Father, deliver us from selfishness and short-sightedness that could ruin our generational blessings, in Jesus' name.*

Laying Godly Foundations:

9. *Lord, help us to build a foundation of righteousness that will outlive us, in Jesus' name.*
10. *Father, let the fear of God govern every decision in our household, in Jesus' name.*
11. *Lord, help us to sow daily seeds of love, obedience, and service that will bear fruit for generations, in Jesus' name.*
12. *Father, let every choice we make today build a lasting legacy of blessing, in Jesus' name.*
13. *Lord, establish Christ as the sure foundation of our family, in Jesus' name.*

Godly Values and Family Vision:

14. *Lord, help us to raise our children in the fear and knowledge of God, in Jesus' name.*
15. *Father, let the values of truth, integrity, and justice be the inheritance of our family, in Jesus' name.*
16. *Lord, give us wisdom to establish a family vision that honors You, in Jesus' name.*
17. *Father, unite us around a common purpose of serving You as a family, in Jesus' name.*
18. *Lord, let our family vision be passed down faithfully from generation to generation, in Jesus' name.*

19. *Father, let every member of our household live to glorify You and strengthen our family testimony, in Jesus' name.*

Developing Gifts and Skills:

20. *Father, open our eyes to discover and develop the gifts You have given to our family, in Jesus' name.*

21. *Lord, let every talent and ability in our household be cultivated for Your glory, in Jesus' name.*

22. *Father, help us pass down wisdom, knowledge, and skills to the next generation, in Jesus' name.*

23. *Lord, let the gifts and trades in our family never die out but multiply for impact, in Jesus' name.*

Order and Stewardship:

24. *Father, give us wisdom to put our house in order for the sake of future generations, in Jesus' name.*

25. *Lord, help us to be faithful stewards of finances, property, and resources, in Jesus' name.*

26. *Father, let our inheritance bring peace and not strife among our children, in Jesus' name.*

27. *Lord, help us to make provisions that secure stability and continuity in our family, in Jesus' name.*

Family Milestones as Spiritual Foundations:

28. *Lord, let every family milestone—birthdays, weddings, funerals—bring glory to Your name, in Jesus' name.*

29. *Father, may our celebrations always plant seeds of faith in the lives of relatives and guests, in Jesus' name.*

30. *Lord, help us to use every gathering as an opportunity to strengthen family unity and witness Christ, in Jesus' name.*

A Vision of Eternity:

31. *Father, help our family to live daily with eternity in view, making choices that glorify You, in Jesus' name.*

32. *Lord, help us fix our eyes not on earthly possessions but on the eternal inheritance You have prepared for us, in Jesus' name.*

33. *Father, align our family vision with heaven's purpose so that our legacy will endure beyond this world, in Jesus' name.*

34. *Lord, remind us that we are pilgrims on earth and give us grace to live as faithful stewards until the end, in Jesus' name.*

35. *Father, prepare us as a family to inherit eternal life and reign with Christ forever, in Jesus' name.*

Prophetic Blessings on the Family:

36. *Father, bless the marriages in our family with love, unity, and faithfulness, in Jesus' name.*
37. *Lord, release godly spouses for our sons and daughters and let their unions bring glory to Your name, in Jesus' name.*
38. *Father, open doors of gainful employment and career advancement for every job-seeker in our family, in Jesus' name.*
39. *Lord, bless the work of our hands and cause us to excel in our careers and businesses, in Jesus' name.*
40. *Father, release divine health and strength over every member of our family, in Jesus' name.*
41. *Lord, heal every sickness and disease in our household and restore us to wholeness, in Jesus' name.*
42. *Father, open doors of favor, opportunities, and breakthroughs for our family, in Jesus' name.*
43. *Lord, let every closed door against our progress swing open by divine intervention, in Jesus' name.*
44. *Father, let the heavens over our family remain open for blessings, provision, and answered prayers, in Jesus' name.*
45. *Lord, release showers of abundance and divine visitation upon our household, in Jesus' name.*
46. *Father, raise men and women of prayer, power, and influence from our family to serve You faithfully, in Jesus' name.*
47. *Lord, anoint our children to become preachers, missionaries, and leaders in Your kingdom, in Jesus' name.*
48. *Father, bless the ministry of our family and make us vessels of transformation to our community and nation, in Jesus' name.*
49. *Lord, satisfy our parents with long life, good health, and peace in their old age, in Jesus' name.*
50. *Father, prosper every project our family undertakes and establish the work of our hands, in Jesus' name.*

Conclusion

I join you to celebrate God Almighty for carrying you through this impactful thirty-day prayer journey. I know the Lord has blessed you abundantly. He wants to use you as an instrument of revival and restoration in your family, Church, community, and the nations. Give yourself entirely to Him.

I counsel you to protect God's precious oil released on your life cautiously. Stay away from sin, become an avid reader, meditate daily on the living Word, share the Good News with others, become a distributor of God's blessings, practice fasting, and remain heavenly conscious.

Your garment will always be white and your head will never lack oil, in Jesus' name (Ecclesiastes 9:8).

Share your testimonies with us via WhatsApp: (+237) 681.722.404

The Restoration House Project

The construction of The Restoration House is currently underway. It is located in Tsinga Village, near the Olembe Stadium in Yaoundé, Cameroon, along the road to Soa.

This modern complex will feature a 1,200-seat auditorium, administrative offices, a multimedia center, a publishing house, and a guest facility. It is designed to serve as the headquarters of the Christian Restoration Network (CRN) – a center for prayer and intercession, discipleship training, leadership development, ministerial coaching, and the humanitarian initiatives of CRN.

1) **Partner with us today** as we labor to realize this dream for God's Kingdom. For partnership, call: (+237) 674.495.895/ 699.902.618 or WhatsApp: 674.495.895.

2) **Send your gifts to:**
   ECOBANK Acc. No.: 0040812604565101
   ORANGE MONEY: 696.565.864
   MTN MOBILE MONEY: 652.382.693

Endnotes

[1] https://www.christianity.com/wiki/bible/what-is-a-covenant-biblical-meaning-and-importance-today.html (consulté le 14 juin 2025).

[2] Barna Group, *Parents and Pastors : Partners in Gen Z Discipleship* (Ventura, CA : Barna Group, 2022), https://www.barna.com/research/parents-and-pastors-partners-in-gen-z-discipleship/ (consulté en juin 2025).

[3] *« An Amazing Secret to Marriage Success, »* Encompass Connection Center, https://www.encompasscc.org/blog/an-amazing-secret-to-marriage-success (consulté le 11 août 2025).

[4] Barna Group, *How Teens Around the World View the Bible*, The Open Generation (Ventura, CA: Barna Group, 2022), *https://www.barna.com/research/open-generation-perceptions* (consulté le 11 août 2025).

[5] https://www.google.com/search?q=statistics+on+the+probability+of+children+of+those+who+follow+Jesus+Christ+sincerely+ending+up+as+genuine+believers (consulté le 23 juillet 2025).

[6] https://www.google.com/search?q=statistics+of+childrne+of+parents+who+are+in+Church+but+not+committed+to+the+faith+becoming+genuine+believers (consulté le 23 juillet 2025).

[7] ExploringJudaism.org. *Jewish Obligations of Parents to Children*. https://www.exploringjudaism.org/learning/jewish-obligations-of-parents-to-children (consulté le 20 juillet 2025).

[8] habad.org. *Teaching Children Responsibility*. https://www.chabad.org/library/article_cdo/aid/745470/jewish/Teaching-Children-Responsibility.htm (consulté le 25 juin 2025).

[9] Kaiser Jr., Walter C., *The Old Testament Documents: Are They Reliable and Relevant?*, Zondervan, 2001.

Publications by Christian Restoration Network

1- Prayer Storm Daily Prayer Guide (monthly devotional)
2- Power Must Change Hands Vol.1: Dealing with Evil Foundations
3- Power Must Change Hands Vol.2: Pursue Overtake and Recover All
4- Power Must Change Hands Vol.3: Jesus Christ Must Reign
5- Power Must Change Hands Vol.4: Arise and Shine
6- Power Must Change Hands Vol.5: Family Restoration 1
7- Power Must Change Hands Vol.6: Family Restoration 2
8- Power Must Change Hands Vol.7: Raise an Altar
9- Power Must Change Hands Vol.8: Commanding Total Victory
10- Power Must Change Hands Vol.9: Enjoying Your Freedom in Christ
11- Power Must Change Hands Vol.10: Supernatural Breakthrough
12- Festival of Fire Series No.1: Let the Fire Fall
13- Festival of Fire Series No.2: Anointed Vessels
14- Festival of Fire Series No.3: God's Agent of Revival
15- Festival of Fire Series No.4: Raising Altars of Restoration
16- Festival of Fire Series No.5: Foundations of a Blessed Family
17- Dominion
18- Divine Overflow
19- Unbreakable
20- Higher Heights
21- Arresting Family Destroyers 1
22- Arresting Family Destroyers 2
23- Praying Like Jesus
24- Conquering the Giant Called Poverty
25- Generous Living
26- Bind the Strongman
27- Personal and Family Deliverance
28- A Difference by Fire
29- Your Time for Divine Expansion
30- Jesus Our Jubilee
31- The Choice of a Friend
32- Christians and Politics
33- A Dynamic Prayer Life

34- Restoring Broken Foundations
35- Restoration by Fire
36- Divine Detox: God's Way to Cleanse, Heal, and Renew Your Body

NB: Our publications are in English and French.

For copies, contact your local books store or direct your request to:

Prayer Storm Team
P.O. Box 5018 Nkwen, Bamenda
Tel.: (237) 677.436.964 or 679.465.717 or 675.686.005
crnprayerstorm@gmail.com

NB: All our books are available in hard copies and soft copies.

Prayer Storm Online Store:
With MTN or Orange Mobile Money *(for those in Cameroon)* and E-Wallet *(for those abroad)*, you can easily obtain the electronic version of this book and other CRN publications via **www.amazon.com** at
https://shorturl.at/pqxyT or
www.christianrestorationnetwork.org/our-bookstore.
https://goo.gl/ktf3rT
Contact (237) 679.465.717 or
prayerstorm@christianrestorationnetwork.org

www.ingramcontent.com/pod-product-compliance
Lightning Source LLC
Chambersburg PA
CBHW071957090426
42740CB00011B/1985